Great Passenger Ships of the World

Volume 2: 1913–1923

Vaterland

Great Passenger Ships of the World

Volume 2: 1913 –1923

Arnold Kludas

Translated by Charles Hodge

Patrick Stephens, Wellingborough

First published in Germany under the title
Die Grossen Passagierschiffe der Welt
First published in Great Britain June 1976
Reprinted July 1986

British Library Cataloguing in Publication Data

Kludas, Arnold
    Great passenger ships of the world.
    Vol. 2: 1913-1923
    1. Passenger ships—History—Pictorial works
    I. Title   II. Die grossen Passagierschiffe
    der Welt. *English*
    387.2'43'09034   VM381

    ISBN 0-85059-242-9

*Patrick Stephens Limited is part of the
Thorsons Publishing Group.*

Printed and bound in Great Britain.

Foreword

This second volume of my documentation covers the development of the large passenger ship during the decade 1913-1923. In this relatively short period we see a decline in the tonnage competition between the leading North Atlantic shipping companies which had been leading to newer and newer maritime superlatives. The ships of the Imperator-class, introduced into service from 1913 onwards, remained for 20 years the largest in the world. This development had been halted by the First World War which not only crippled nearly all passenger services but also claimed numerous victims among the great liners and the people serving and travelling aboard them. Many ships which were not completed until after the war had broken out, including the intended flagships of the British and Dutch merchant fleets, the Britannic and the Statendam, were sunk without ever having made a voyage with fare-paying passengers. After the Armistice, the reconstruction of passenger services was commenced.

For the time being, the German flag played no part in international passenger shipping, although Germany had attained a very high second place by 1914. Large passenger ships were introduced on the traditional routes by other nations, such as Italy, which had scarcely been represented up to 1914. The turbulent decade which ended with 1923 was, however, to be followed by portents of stability.

Arnold Kludas
Hamburg: November, 1975.

Explanatory Notes

All passenger ships ever launched having a gross registered tonnage (GRT) of over 10,000 are presented in the five volumes of this work. This the second volume deals with the period from 1913 to 1923.

The ships are arranged chronologically, with the exception of sister-ships or groups of ships which have been placed together regardless of exact chronology. The chronological order of the individual sections has been determined from the launching date of the first ship of the class or group. The technical/historical biography of each ship appears under the name with which the ship first entered service. This applies also if the ship sailed later under other names and for other shipping companies. This rule is departed from only in exceptional circumstances. To trace a particular ship the reader is recommended to use the Index of Ships' Names, pages 238/240.

In cases where ships have been renamed these are included after the first name in each case, as a further help in tracing all the later names, each with the year of the name change. The following is a guide to the technical and historical information concerning the ships.

I. Technical Data

The information given in the paragraph on technical data applies fundamentally to the date when the ship first went into service as a passenger carrier. Planned specifications are given in the case of incompleted ships for which at their respective stages of construction these had not been fully decided upon. Alterations affecting technical data are noted with historical data against the appropriate dates.

Dimensions Length overall × moulded breadth in metres rounded off to one place of decimals, followed by the equivalent in feet, the length to the nearest whole number and breadth to one place of decimals. Length overall has been adopted in preference to other length measurements. It was found that recorded registered length and length between perpendiculars could vary from time to time and from place to place.

Propulsion Type of machinery, constructor. Where the shipbuilder has not been responsible for the propelling machinery, its constructor is given. The abbreviations III or IV exp eng indicate triple or quadruple expansion (steam) engines.

Power The figure of horse power given is the highest performance attainable by the engines in normal service. The different methods of measuring horse power, according to the form of propulsion, are as follows:
IHP = indicated horse power, unit of measurement for reciprocating steam engines and internal combustion engines.
SHP = shaft horse power, for turbine machinery and internal combustion engines.
BHP = brake horse power, unit of measurement for internal combustion engines.
The horse power figures, thus arrived at through different methods, cannot necessarily be compared with each other. While BHP and SHP are practically identical, their relationship to the indicated horse power (IHP) is in the region of 4:5. 8,000 SHP is thus equivalent to 10,000 IHP.

Speed Service speed is given in knots. This is followed, as far as can be established, by the highest speed achieved on trials with the engines running at maximum power.

Passengers On nearly all ships the passenger accommodation and the number of berths for each class were frequently altered. Even if it were still possible today to establish all these changes exactly, the necessary effort would not justify the value of the figures thus obtained. One can come to completely different conclusions however correct the figures, for sofa-berths or emergency beds may or may not have been included. The information on alterations to passenger accommodation therefore is limited to really significant modifications, as far as it has been possible to determine them. In the case of many ships built before 1914, it is often impossible to differentiate clearly between third class and steerage. The standard in the lowest-priced classes of passenger accommodation varied from ship to ship, and between owners and routes, from large primitive mass dormitories (which could be used alternatively for the carriage of cargo) to relatively comfortable equipped rooms with a moderate number of beds. On many ships these variations existed side by side under the general description of 'third class'. One can reasonably assume that on a three-class ship with a large third class capacity, a considerable number of the latter passengers would be accommodated in dormitories. The description 'steerage' is therefore appropriate.

Crew Crew-strength also was subject to alteration, as for instance when a ship was converted from coal to oil-firing, or when the passenger capacity was changed. Changes in crew-strength have not been noted. Unfortunately it has not been possible to determine crew-strength for every ship.

II. Historical Data

The historical information reflects in chronological order the career of the ship, giving all important events and facts.

Owners In the ships' biographies, shipowners are indicated throughout by what are considered to be the accepted short-forms in English-speaking countries. Nevertheless, a selected short-form may not itself be based on an English translation of a non-English title, for instance: Nippon Yusen KK, CGT, etc. It is assumed that Cie, Cia, AG, SA, etc, will be as familiar to readers as are such English abbreviations as SN, SS, Co, Corp, etc. After the name of a shipowner, the location mentioned in each case is the ship's home port, which is not necessarily where the shipowner has

Contents

his head office.
An alphabetical list of all shipowners with their complete styles is included as an appendix to Volume V.

Builders Like shipowners, builders are noted throughout by their accepted short-forms, and are listed alphabetically with their complete styles in Volume V.

Completion Completion-date is the date of commencement of trials.

Routes Ports of call are omitted from the information concerning routes.

The Imperator-Class

Turbine steamer *Imperator*
Hamburg-America Line,
Hamburg

1921 Berengaria

Builders: 'Vulcan', Hamburg
Yard no: 314
52,117 GRT; 277.1 × 29.9 m /
909 × 98.1 ft; Turbines,
AEG-Vulcan; Quadruple screw;
74,000 SHP; 23, max 24 kn;
Passengers: 908 1st class, 972 2nd
class, 942 3rd class, 1,772 steerage;
Crew: 1,180.

1912 May 23: Launched.
1913 Apr 22: Completed. Until
1914 the largest ship in the world.
May 23: Delivered.
Jun 10: Maiden voyage Cuxhaven-
New York.

Nov: Alterations to improve
stability. Funnels shortened by
about nine feet.
1914 Aug: Laid up at Hamburg for
the duration of the war.
1919 Apr 27: Last voyage from
Hamburg, to be handed over to the
USA.
May 5: US Navy transport.
Aug: Laid up at New York.
1920 Feb: Handed over to Great
Britain. Chartered by Cunard Line
from the Shipping Controller.
Feb 21: First voyage Liverpool-New
York.
Jun 6: Southampton-New York
service.
1921 Feb: Sold to Cunard Line.
Renamed *Berengaria*.
Sep: Refit commenced by

Armstrong, Whitworth & Co at
Newcastle which lasted until May,
1922. 52,226 GRT. Passengers:
972 1st class, 630 2nd class, 606 3rd
class, 515 tourist class. Oil-firing.
1934 Feb: Cunard Line and White
Star Line amalgamated to form
Cunard-White Star Line.
1938 Mar 3: The *Berengaria* was
badly damaged while at New York
as a result of a fire in her passenger
accommodation. She returned to
Southampton without passengers
and was laid up.
Nov 7: Sold to be broken up at
Jarrow.
1939 The ship scrapped down to
her double bottom.
1946 What was left towed to
Rosyth and broken up.

1

2

3

1 *The Hamburg-America Liner*
Imperator *towards the end of her*
fitting out.

2 *The departure of the* Imperator *for*
trials.
3 *The Cunard liner* Berengaria *ex*
Imperator *after her 1922 refit.*

Turbine steamer *Vaterland*
Hamburg-America Line,
Hamburg

1917 *Leviathan*

Builders: Blohm & Voss, Hamburg
Yard no: 212
54,282 GRT; 289.2 × 30.5 m /
948 × 100 ft; Turbines, Parsons-
B & V; Quadruple screw; 90,400
SHP; 23.5, max 25.8 kn;
Passengers: 752 1st class, 535 2nd
class, 850 3rd class, 1,772 steerage;
Crew: 1,234.

1913 Apr 3: Launched.
1914 Apr 29: Completed. Largest
ship in the world until 1922, and
from 1923 to 1931.
May 14: Maiden voyage
Cuxhaven-New York.
Aug: Interned at New York.
1917 Apr: Due to threat of seizure
by the USA the crew damaged the
engines and the boilers.
Apr 4: Seized by the USA.
Jul 25: After repairs, US Navy
transport.
Sep 6: Renamed *Leviathan*.
1919 Sep: Laid up at New York,
handed over to US Shipping
Board.
1922 Feb: To Newport News for
reconstruction as passenger ship by
Newport News Shipbuilding &
Dry Dock Co.
1923 Jun 19: The *Leviathan,* now
measured at 59,956 GRT,
completed her trials with an
average speed of 27.48 kn.
Passengers: 970 1st class, 542 2nd
class, 944 3rd class, 935 4th class.
Later reduced to 940 1st class, 666
tourist class, 1,402 3rd class.
Jul 4: First voyage New
York-Southampton for United
States Lines.
1931 Tonnage reduced to 48,932
GRT. This astonishing change in
the measurement was achieved
without external rebuilding, but
through manipulation of
measuring regulations. In 1923
fashion had favoured 'the biggest
ship in the world', which the
Majestic, ex *Bismarck,* had been,
de facto, since 1922. The purpose
of this reduction was to save
harbour dues.

1932 Laid up.
1934 Four more voyages to
Southampton.
Sep: Laid up at New York.
1937 Dec: Sold for breaking-up to
Metal Industries Ltd, Rosyth, and
T.W. Ward, Sheffield.
1938 Jan 26: The *Leviathan* left
New York on course for Rosyth,
where she arrived on Feb 14.

4 *The* Vaterland *was the largest
passenger ship to enter service under
the German flag.*
5 *The* Leviathan, *ex* Vaterland, *as US
Navy transport.*
6 *The* Leviathan *during her refitting as
a passenger ship at Newport News in
1922.*
7 *United States liner* Leviathan.

4

5

6

7

Turbine steamer *Bismarck*
Hamburg-America Line,
Hamburg

1922 *Majestic;* 1937 *Caledonia*

Builders: Blohm & Voss, Hamburg
Yard no: 214
56,551 GRT; 291.4 × 30.5 m /
956 × 100 ft; Turbines, Parsons-
B & V; Quadruple screw; 86,000
SHP; 23.5, max 24.75 kn;
Passengers: 750 1st class, 545 2nd
class, 850 3rd class; Crew: 1,000.

1914 Jun 20: Launched.
Aug: Work on ship ceased for the
duration of the war.
1919 Jun 28: Germany signed the
Treaty of Versailles, under which
the *Bismarck* was to be handed
over to Great Britain. Building
continued under British
supervision.

1920 Oct 5: Completion
considerably delayed by fire.
1921 Feb: The British
Government sold the *Bismarck* and
the *Imperator* together to Cunard
Line and White Star Line. The
latter took over the *Bismarck*.
1922 Mar 28: Completed. The
largest ship in the world.
Apr 1: Start of trials, which lasted
a total of 10 days. She was then
renamed *Majestic*.
May 10: Maiden voyage
Southampton-New York.
1934 Feb: White Star Line and
Cunard amalgamated to form
Cunard-White Star Ltd.
1936 Feb: Laid up at
Southampton.
May 15: Sold for breaking up to
T.W. Ward. Resold to British
Admiralty and refitted as training

ship for 2,000 boys by
Thornycroft, Southampton.
1937 Apr 23: At Rosyth as
stationary training ship *Caledonia*.
1939 Sep: Refit as transport
planned.
Sep 29: HMS *Caledonia* was
completely burned out and sank
on an even keel in shallow water.
1940 Mar: Sold for scrap to T.W.
Ward. Broken up on the spot
down to the waterline.
1943 Jul 17: Remainder of wreck
was raised and towed to
Inverkeithing, where it was
scrapped.

8/9 *The* Bismarck *during trials.*

8

10 *The* Majestic *ex* Bismarck *was the largest ship in the world until 1935.*

14 Alsatian and Calgarian

Turbine steamer *Alsatian*
Allan Line, Glasgow

1919 Empress of France

Builders: Beardmore, Glasgow
Yard no: 509
18,485 GRT; 182.9 × 22.0 m /
600 × 72.2 ft; Turbines, Parsons-
Beardmore; Quadruple screw;
21,400 SHP; 18, max 20 kn;
Passengers: 263 1st class, 506 2nd
class, 976 3rd class; Crew: 500.

1913 Mar 22: Launched.
Dec: Completed.
1914 Jan 17: Maiden voyage
Liverpool-Halifax-St John.
Aug 7: Auxiliary cruiser in 10th
Cruiser Squadron.
Dec: Flagship of Squadron.
1917 Jul: Allan Line taken over by
Canadian Pacific.
1919 Feb: To Beardmore,
Glasgow for overhaul and refitting
as passenger ship.
Apr 4: Renamed *Empress of
France*.
Sep 26: First voyage
Liverpool-Quebec.
1922 May 30: First voyage
Hamburg-Quebec.
1924 Converted to oil-firing, by
Beardmore.
1927 Oct: Southampton-Quebec
service.
1928 Oct 31: From Southampton
to Vancouver; trans-Pacific service
until Oct 1929.
1929 Southampton-Quebec service
again.
1931 Sep 28: Laid up on the Clyde.
1934 Oct 20: Sold for breaking-up
to W.H. Arnott Young & Co.
Nov 24: Arrived at Dalmuir.

Turbine steamer *Calgarian*
Allan Line, Glasgow

Builders: Fairfield, Glasgow
Yard no: 487
17,521 GRT; 179.8 × 21.4 m /
590 × 70.2 ft; Turbines, Parsons-
Fairfield; Quadruple screw; 21,000
SHP; 18, max 21.6 kn; Passengers:
200 1st class, 450 2nd class, 1,000
3rd class; Crew: 500.

1913 Apr 19: Launched.
1914 Mar 16: Completed.
May: Maiden voyage Liverpool-
St John.
Sep 15: Auxiliary cruiser in Royal
Navy.
1917 Jul: Allan Line taken over by
Canadian Pacific.
1918 Mar 1: The *Calgarian* was
torpedoed and sunk by the
German submarine *U 19* off
Rathlin Island. 49 dead.

1

2

3

1 *Allan liner* Alsatian, *in her time the largest ship on the Canada route.*

2 The Empress of France, *ex* Alsatian.

3 *After four years of service, the* Calgarian *was sunk in 1918 by a German submarine.*

The A-Class of Cunard Line

Steamship *Andania*
Cunard Line, Liverpool

Builders: Scott's, Greenock
Yard no: 446
13,405 GRT; 164.6 × 19.5 m /
540 × 64 ft; IV exp eng, Scott's;
Twin screw; 8,500 IHP; 14.5 kn;
Passengers: 520 2nd class, 1,620
3rd class; Crew: 289.

1913 Mar 23: Launched.
Jul: Completed.
Jul 17: Maiden voyage
Liverpool-Montreal, then
London-Montreal. In winter,
London-Halifax and Boston
service.
1914 Oct 14: Troop transport until
March 18 1916.
1916 Mar 18: First voyage
London-New York.
1918 Jan 27: The *Andania* was
torpedoed and sunk by the German
submarine *U 46* two nautical miles
north of the Rathlin Island
lighthouse. Seven dead.

Steamship *Alaunia*
Cunard Line, Liverpool

Builders: Scott's, Greenock
Yard no: 447
13,405 GRT; 164.6 × 19.5 m /
540 × 64 ft; IV exp eng, Scott's;
Twin screw; 8,500 IHP; 14.5 kn;
Passengers: 520 2nd class, 1,620
3rd class; Crew: 289.

1913 Jun 9: Launched.
Nov: Completed.
Nov 27: Maiden voyage
Liverpool-Boston, then
London-Boston service in winter
and London-Montreal in summer.
1914 Aug: Troop transport.
1916 May 11: First voyage
London-New York.
Oct 19: The *Alaunia* struck a mine
in the English Channel two
nautical miles south of the
Royal Sovereign lightship and
sank. Two dead.

Turbine steamer *Aurania*
Cunard Line, Liverpool

Builders: Swan, Hunter & Wigham
Richardson, Newcastle
Yard no: 965
13,936 GRT; 164.6 × 19.9 m /
540 × 65.3 ft; Geared turbines,
Wallsend Slipway; Twin screw;
9,000 SHP; 15 kn; Passengers: 506
2nd class, 1,650 3rd class; Crew:
291.

1916 Jul 16: Launched.
1917 Mar 28: Maiden voyage
Newcastle-New York. Service as
transport on the North Atlantic.
1918 Feb 4: The *Aurania* was
torpedoed by the German
submarine *UB 67* 15 nautical miles
north of Inishtrahull (Ireland).
During an attempt to tow the badly
damaged ship to port, she ran
aground on submerged rocks off
Tobermory and became a total
loss. Eight dead.

3

1 *The* Andania *being fitted out at
Greenock. In the foreground is the
British battleship* Ajax.
2 *Cunard liner* Alaunia.
3 *Only completed in 1917, the* Aurania
*was stranded in February, 1918, after a
torpedo attack.*

Turbine steamer *Albania*
Cunard Line, Liverpool

1930 *California*

Builders: Scott's, Greenock
Yard no: 479
12,768 GRT; 164.3 × 19.5 m /
539 × 64 ft; Geared turbines,
Brown-Curtis-Scott's; Twin screw;
6,800 SHP; 13 kn; Passengers: 480
cabin class.

1914 Keel laid down as fourth
A-Class ship.
Construction was then ceased
during the war, but later continued
on governmental order, as
freighter. After the war Cunard
planned passenger cabins for the
steerage section.

1920 Apr 17: Launched.
Dec: Completed.
1921 Jan 18: Maiden voyage
Liverpool-New York.
1922 Apr 20: First voyage
Liverpool-Montreal.
1925 Laid up.
1930 Jan: Sold to Nav Libera
Triestina, Trieste. Renamed
California. Reconstruction of
passenger accommodation: 130 1st
class, 30 2nd class. 12,951 GRT.
Dec 11: First voyage
Genoa-Seattle.
1935 The *California* was refitted as
a hospital ship during the
Abyssinian War.
1937 As a result of the state
reorganisation of Italian shipping,

the Nav Libera Triestina was
dissolved. The *California* was now
managed as a hospital ship by
Lloyd Triestino.
1941 Aug 11: Sunk by British
torpedo aircraft off Syracuse.

4

5

4 *The fourth ship of the class, the*
Albania, *was to have been completed as
a freighter during the First World War.*
5 *Libera Triestina liner* California, *ex*
Albania.

Steamship *Lutetia*
Cie Sudatlantique, Bordeaux

Builders: Penhoët, St Nazaire
Yard no: 65
14,561 GRT; 182.8 × 19.5 m /
600 × 64 ft; III exp eng plus low
pressure turbines, Penhoët;
Quadruple screw; 26,000 IHP; 20
kn; Passengers: 300 1st class, 110
2nd class, 80 3rd class, 600
steerage; Crew: 410.

1913 Mar 23: Launched.
Oct 15: Completed.
Nov 1: Maiden voyage
Bordeaux-La Plata ports.
1914 Aug: Troop transport.
1915 Dec: Fitted out as auxiliary
cruiser.
1916 Entered service as hospital
ship for a few months, then troop
transport again.

1919 Released from naval service.
Refitted as passenger ship at La
Seyne. Passengers: 460 1st class,
130 2nd class, 90 3rd class, 450
steerage. 14,654 GRT.
1920 Oct 2: First post-war voyage
Bordeaux-La Plata.
1927 Converted to oil-firing by
Penhoët at St Nazaire. While in
dock, the ship suffered such
pressure on her side during a storm
on the night June 15/16 that she
sank. The badly damaged vessel
was raised on June 23.
1930 Passenger accommodation
altered: 212 1st class, 114 2nd
class, 86 3rd class, 500 steerage.
1931 Aug: Laid up in Bordeaux.
1937 Nov: Sold for breaking-up.
1938 Jan 28: The *Lutetia* left
Bordeaux on course for Blyth,
where she was broken up.

1 *Before the First World War the*
Lutetia *was the fastest ship on the
South American route.*

1

Steamship *Gallia*
Cie Sudatlantique, Bordeaux

Builders: F et Ch de la
Méditerranée, La Seyne
Yard no: 1056
14,966 GRT; 182.9 × 19.1 m /
600 × 62.7 ft; III exp eng plus low
pressure turbine from hull
builders; Triple screw; 26,000 IHP;
20 kn; Passengers: 300 1st class,
106 2nd class, 80 3rd class, 600
steerage; Crew: 410.

1913 Mar 26: Launched.
Oct: Completed.
Nov 29: Maiden voyage Bordeaux-
La Plata ports.
1914 Aug: Auxiliary cruiser in
French navy. Later troop
transport.
1916 Oct 4: The *Gallia,* full to
capacity with troops, was
torpedoed by the German
submarine *U 35* 35 nautical miles
west of Sardinia, and sank very
quickly. More than 600 dead.

Steamship *Massilia*
Cie Sudatlantique, Bordeaux

Builders: F et Ch de la
Méditerranée, La Seyne
Yard no: 1061
15,147 GRT; 182.9 × 19.5 m /
600 × 64 ft; III exp eng plus low
pressure turbines from builders;
Quadruple screw; 26,000 IHP; 20
max 21 kn; Passengers: 464 1st
class, 129 2nd class, 98 3rd class,
350 steerage; Crew: 410.

1914 Apr 30: Launched.
Construction ceased during war.
1920 Sep 23: Completed.
Oct 8: Delivered.
Oct 30: Maiden voyage Bordeaux-
La Plata ports.
1928 Converted to oil-firing by
Penhoët at St Nazaire. Bridge deck
altered. 15,363 GRT.
1930 Passenger accommodation
altered: 231 1st class, 71 2nd class,
88 3rd class, 456 steerage.
1940 Apr: Troop transport.
Jun 18: The *Massilia* took 150
members of the French
government from Bordeaux to
Casablanca. Afterwards laid up in
Marseille.
1944 Sunk by German troops off
the Basin Mirabeau in order to
block the harbour.
The wreck was raised and scrapped
after the war.

2 The torpedoing of the Gallia *in 1916
claimed over 600 lives.*
3 The building of the Massilia *was
interrupted for five years by the First
World War. A fourth ship planned for
this class, intended as the* Gergovia,
was never built.

Steamship *Katori Maru*
Nippon Yusen KK, Tokyo

Builders: Mitsubishi, Nagasaki
Yard no: 230
10,513 GRT; 158.5 × 18.2 m /
520 × 59.7 ft; III exp eng plus low
pressure turbine, Mitsubishi;
Triple screw; 11,500 IHP; 15, max
16.7 kn; Passengers: 120 1st class,
60 2nd class, 200 3rd class; Crew:
160.

1913 Mar 30: Launched.
Sep 11: Completed. Entered
Japan-Europe service.
1917 Sep: First voyage in
trans-Pacific service Japan-USA.
9,834 GRT.
1922 Mar: Japan-Europe service
again.
1941 Dec 23: The *Katori Maru*
was torpedoed and sunk by a Dutch
submarine off Kuching, Sarawak.

Steamship *Kashima Maru*
Nippon Yusen KK, Tokyo

1938 *Kasima Maru*

Builders: Kawasaki, Kobe
Yard no: 362
10,599 GRT; 159.1 × 18.1 m /
522 × 59.4 ft; III exp eng,
Kawasaki; Twin screw; 11,000
IHP; 15, max 16.5 kn; Passengers:
120 1st class, 60 2nd class, 200 3rd
class; Crew: 160.

1913 Launched.
Oct 1: Completed. Japan-Europe
service.
1917 Sep: First voyage in
trans-Pacific service Japan-USA.
9,905 GRT.
1922 Japan-Europe service again.
1938 Transliteration corrected to
Kasima Maru.
1943 Sep 27: The *Kasima Maru*
was torpedoed and sunk by the
American submarine *Bonefish* 200
nautical miles east of Saigon.

Steamship *Suwa Maru*
Nippon Yusen KK, Tokyo

Builders: Mitsubishi, Nagasaki
Yard no: 236
10,927 GRT; 158.8 × 19.1 m /
521 × 62.6 ft; III exp eng,
Mitsubishi; Twin screw; 11,000
IHP; 15, max 16.5 kn; Passengers:
122 1st class, 53 2nd class, 336 3rd
class; Crew: 160.

1914 Mar 29: Launched.
Sep 10: Delivered. Japan-Europe
service.
1917 Sep: First voyage in
trans-Pacific service Japan-USA.
1922 Mar: Japan-Europe service
again.
During the '30s, the 3rd class
accommodation was reduced to 50
passengers.
1943 Mar 28: Sailing as troop
transport in the Pacific, the *Suwa
Maru* was torpedoed by the US
submarine *Tunny* and had to be
run aground near Wake. On April
5 the ship was completely destroyed
by a torpedo attack from the US
submarines *Seadragon* and
Finback.

1 *Steamship* Katori Maru.

2 *The* Kashima Maru *with the NYK funnel markings introduced in the '20s.*
3 *Nippon Yusen Liner* Suwa Maru *during trials.*

Steamship *Fushimi Maru*
Nippon Yusen KK, Tokyo

1938 *Husimi Maru*

Builders: Mitsubishi, Nagasaki
Yard no: 237
10,940 GRT; 160.0 × 19.1 m /
525 × 62.6 ft; III exp eng,
Mitsubishi; Twin screw; 11,000
IHP; 15, max 16.5 kn; Passengers:
122 1st class, 60 2nd class, 330 3rd
class; Crew: 160.

1914 Jun 28: Launched.
Nov 23: Delivered. Japan-Europe
service.
1917 First voyage in trans-Pacific
service, Japan-USA.
1922 Japan-Europe service again.
1938 Transliteration corrected to
Husimi Maru.
1943 Feb 1: Torpedoed and sunk
off the Honshu coast by the US
submarine *Tarpon*.

Steamship *Yasaka Maru*
Nippon Yusen KK, Tokyo

Builders: Kawasaki, Kobe
Yard no: 369
10,932 GRT; 159.5 × 19.1 m /
523 × 62.6 ft; III exp eng,
Kawasaki; Twin screw; 11,000
IHP; 15, max 16.5 kn; Passengers:
122 1st class, 60 2nd class, 330 3rd
class; Crew: 160.

1914 Completed. Japan-Europe
service.
1915 Dec 21: The *Yasaka Maru*
was torpedoed and sunk by the
German submarine *U 38* 60
nautical miles from Port Said. The
crew and passengers were able to
escape in the lifeboats.

4 *The* Fushimi Maru, *which entered
service in November 1914.*
5 *After one year of service, the*
Yasaka Maru *was torpedoed in the
Mediterranean.*

The Aquitania

Turbine steamer *Aquitania*
Cunard Line, Liverpool

Builders: Brown, Clydebank
Yard no: 409
45,647 GRT; 274.8 × 29.6 m /
901 × 97.1 ft; Turbines,
Parsons-Brown; Quadruple screw;
62,000 SHP; 23, max 24 kn;
Passengers: 618 1st class, 614 2nd
class, 1,998 3rd class; Crew: 972.

1913 Apr 21: Launched.
1914 May 10: Completed.
May 30: Maiden voyage Liverpool-
New York.
Aug: Auxiliary cruiser in Royal
Navy.
Sep: Taken out of service, as the
use of such large ships as auxiliary
cruisers had become questionable.

1915 Spring: Troop transport to
the Dardanelles. Then served as
hospital ship in the Mediterranean.
1917 Laid up at Liverpool.
1918 Troop transport
USA-France.
1919 Jun 14: First post-war voyage
Southampton-New York.
Nov: To Newcastle for conversion
to oil-firing by Armstrong,
Whitworth.
1920 Jul 18: Explosion in engine
room during first voyage after
conversion. One dead.
Aug: Southampton-New York
service again.
1926 Passenger accommodation:
610 1st class, 950 2nd class, 640
tourist class.
1939 Nov 21: Troop transport.

1948 May: First voyage in
Southampton-Halifax service as
one-class ship.
1949 Dec: Sold for breaking-up to
British Iron & Steel Corp.
1950 Feb 21: Arrived at Faslane;
broken up by Metal Industries.

1/2 *Cunard liner* Aquitania *during trials.*
3 *The* Aquitania *as troop transport in November 1944.*

1

2

3

Steamship *Gelria*
Royal Holland Lloyd, Amsterdam

1935 *Gradisca*

Builders: Stephen, Glasgow
Yard no: 454
13,868 GRT; 170.7 × 20.0 m /
560 × 65.6 ft; IV exp eng,
Stephen; Twin screw; 12,000 IHP;
16, max 17.5 kn; Passengers: 250
1st class, 230 2nd class, 140 3rd
class, 900 steerage; Crew 330.

1913 May 20: Launched.
Oct 8: Completed.
Nov 5: Maiden voyage
Amsterdam-La Plata ports.
1916 Laid up at Amsterdam after
torpedoing of sister ship *Tubantia*.
1919 Mar 12: First post-war
voyage Amsterdam-La Plata.
1921 Chartered to Rotterdam
Lloyd for one voyage to Dutch East
Indies.
1928 Converted to oil-firing. The
passenger accommodation had
been reduced earlier to 233 1st
class, 350 2nd class and 704 3rd
class.
1931 Nov 5: Laid up due to world
depression.

1933 Chartered to Argentinian
government. Plans for service as
exhibition ship not realised,
however.
1934 Apr 21: Laid up again at
Amsterdam.
1935 Aug: Sold to Italian
government.
Nov: Renamed *Gradisca,* managed
by Lloyd Triestino, Trieste. Used
as troop transport in Abyssinian
War, occasionally as hospital ship.
After the Abyssinian War, some
service voyages to East Africa.
1940 Hospital ship in the Second
War War.
1943 Oct 3: Following the Italian
capitulation the German Navy took
over the ship in the Mediterranean,
later to be used as a hospital ship.
1944 Oct 28: On a voyage from
Salonika to Trieste with wounded
the fully authenticated *Gradisca*
was held up by a British submarine
and ordered into Alexandria. After
the disembarkation of 1,000 lightly
wounded, the ship was taken to
Algiers.
1945 Jan 20: After lengthy
diplomatic exchanges the *Gradisca*

was returned to Germany but did
not re-enter German service,
becoming a British war prize.
1946 Jan 23: On a voyage from
Port Said to Malta the *Gradisca*
ran aground off the island of
Gavdos.
1947 Jun: Salvaged and laid up at
Venice.
1949 Sold for breaking-up to Soc
Ital Breda, Venice.
1950 Broken up at Venice.

1 *The* Gelria *during her first years of
service.*
2 *The Italian troop transport*
Gradisca, *ex* Gelria.
3 *During the Second World War the*
Gradisca *served as a hospital ship.*

Steamship *Tubantia*
Royal Holland Lloyd, Amsterdam

Builders: Stephen, Glasgow
Yard no: 455
13,911 GRT; 170.7 × 20.0 m /
560 × 65.6 ft; IV exp eng,
Stephen; Twin screw; 12,000 IHP;
16, max 17.5 kn; Passengers: 250
1st class, 230 2nd class, 140 3rd
class, 900 steerage; Crew: 330.

1913 Nov 15: Launched.

1914 Mar 11: Completed.
Apr: Maiden voyage
Amsterdam-La Plata ports.

1916 Mar 16: The *Tubantia* was
torpedoed by the German
submarine *UB 13* near the
Noordhinder lightship, and sank
four and a half hours later.

Passengers and crew were saved by
Dutch rescue vessels.

4 *The* Tubantia. *Her sinking by a
German submarine led to diplomatic
friction between the Netherlands and
Germany.*

4

Steamship *Frederik VIII*
Det Forenede D/S, Copenhagen

Builders: 'Vulcan', Stettin
Yard no: 332
11,850 GRT; 165.8 × 19.0 m /
544 × 62.3 ft; III exp eng, Vulcan;
Twin screw; 10,000 IHP; 17 kn;
Passengers: 100 1st class, 300 2nd
class, 950 3rd class.

1913 May 27: Launched.
Dec: completed.
1914 Feb 5: Maiden voyage
Copenhagen-New York. Passenger
accommodation altered during the
'20s: 218 1st class, 293 2nd class,
696 3rd class.
1935 Dec: Laid up.
1936 Sep: Sold to Hughes,
Bolckow & Co to be broken up.

1937 Broken up at Blyth.

1 Frederick VIII, *the flagship of the
Danish North Atlantic service, with
neutrality markings during the First
World War.*

1

Cap Trafalgar and Cap Polonio

Steamship *Cap Trafalgar*
Hamburg-South America Line,
Hamburg

Builders: Vulcan, Hamburg
Yard no: 334
18,805 GRT; 186.8 × 22.0 m /
613 × 72.2 ft; III exp eng plus low
pressure turbine, Vulcan; Triple
screw; 15,000 IHP; 17, max 17.8
kn; Passengers: 400 1st class, 274
2nd class, 912 3rd class; Crew: 436.

1913 Jul 31: Launched.
1914 Mar 1: Completed.
Mar 10: Maiden voyage
Hamburg-La Plata ports.
Aug 2: The *Cap Trafalgar* reached
Buenos Aires after the outbreak of
war, and awaited orders
concerning service as auxiliary
cruiser.
Aug 18: To Montevideo to coal.
Aug 23: Sailed out to meet the
gunboat *Eber,* which handed over
her weapons to the steamer at sea.
Third funnel removed.
Aug 31: Entered service as
auxiliary cruiser.
Sep 13: After the first unsuccessful voyage, the *Cap
Trafalgar* met up with colliers off
the Brazilian island of Trinidad.
Sep 14: The British auxiliary
cruiser *Carmania* approached, and
coaling was interrupted. After a
battle of nearly two hours, the *Cap
Trafalgar* sank. The British ship
turned away, on fire. There were
nine dead on board the *Carmania,*
and 16 on the German ship. The
survivors from the *Cap Trafalgar*
were picked up by the *Eleonore
Woermann.*

*1/2 Hamburg-South America Line
express steamer* Cap Trafalgar. *After
five months on the South America
service she was fitted out as an auxiliary
cruiser and sunk 14 days later.*

Steamship *Cap Polonio*
Hamburg-South America Line,
Hamburg

1915 *Vineta;* 1915 *Cap Polonio*

Builders: Blohm & Voss, Hamburg
Yard no: 221
20,576 GRT; 201.8 × 22.1 m /
662 × 72.5 ft; III exp eng plus low
pressure turbine, B & V; Triple
screw; 20,000 IHP; 17, max 19 kn;
Passengers: 356 1st class, 250 2nd
class, 949 3rd class; Crew: 460.

1914 Mar 25: Launched.
Aug: Construction halted following
outbreak of war. Fitting out as
auxiliary cruiser commenced at
end of 1914.
Third funnel removed.
1915 Feb 8: Entered service as
auxiliary cruiser *Vineta.*
Feb 10: Intended speed not
achieved on trial run. 17 kn only
just possible.
Feb 14: Taken out of service.
Armament removed, and refitted
as passenger ship. Named *Cap
Polonio* again.

1916 Completed.
1919 Apr 15: Handed over to
Great Britain. Chartered to Union
Castle Line by the Shipping
Controller.
Jun 21: First voyage
Plymouth-Cape Town. Chartered
to P & O Line on return. One round
voyage London-Bombay-London,
then handed back to Shipping
Controller.
1920 Laid up at Liverpool.
Constant trouble with the engines,
which only produced 10-12 kn
despite several overhauls.
1921 Jul 20: Hamburg-South
America Line bought back the *Cap
Polonio.* General overhaul by
Blohm & Voss. Converted to oil-
firing. Engines now gave trouble-
free performance on trials.
1922 Feb 16: First voyage
Hamburg-La Plata ports.
Cruising.
1931 Refit and modernisation of
passenger accommodation. Laid
up at Hamburg because of world
depression.

1933 Sep: Exhibition ship at the
Hamburg Overseas Landing Stage,
then laid up again.
1935 Jun: Sold to be broken up.
Scrapped at the North German
Lloyd Line's repair yard in
Bremerhaven.

3

3 *The* Cap Polonio *during her refit as
an auxiliary cruiser in the winter of
1914/15.*
4 Cap Polonio *on a trial trip in January
1922.*
5 *The* Cap Polonio *in Hamburg
harbour around 1930.*

Steamship *Llanstephan Castle*
Union-Castle Line, London

Builders: Fairfield, Glasgow
Yard no: 494
11,293 GRT; 158.3 × 19.3 m /
519 × 63.3 ft; IV exp eng,
Fairfield; Twin screw; 6,500 IHP;
14, max 15 kn; Passengers: 213 1st
class, 116 2nd class, 100 3rd class;
Crew: 250.

1913 Aug 29: Launched.
1914 Feb: Completed.
London-East Africa service. Used
mostly on the South Africa route
during First World War.
1920 London-East Africa again.
1940 During Second World War
transport for the Ministry of War
Transport and the Royal Indian
Navy.
1947 Sep: First voyage in
London-Round Africa-London
service. Passenger
accommodation: 231 1st class, 198
tourist class.
1952 Mar: Sold for breaking-up to
British Iron & Steel Corp (Salvage)
Ltd.

Steamship *Llandovery Castle*
Union-Castle Line, London

Builders: Barclay, Curle & Co,
Glasgow
Yard no: 504
11,423 GRT; 157.6 × 19.3 m /
517 × 63.3 ft; IV exp eng from
builders; Twin screw; 6,500 IHP;
14, max 15 kn; Passengers: 213 1st
class, 116 2nd class, 100 3rd class;
Crew: 250.

1913 Sep 3: Launched.
1914 Jan: Completed.
London-East Africa service.
Aug: On England-West Africa
route.
1917 Hospital ship.
1918 Jun 27: The hospital ship
Llandovery Castle was torpedoed
and sunk by the German
submarine *U 86* 114 nautical miles
west of Fastnet. 234 dead.

1

2

1 *The* Llanstephan Castle *in Cape Town.*
2 *The* Llandovery Castle, *sunk in June 1918, while serving as a hospital ship.*

Steamship *Orduña*
Pacific Steam Nav Co, Liverpool

Builders: Harland & Wolff, Belfast
Yard no: 438
15,507 GRT; 173.4 × 20.5 m /
569 × 67.3 ft; III exp eng plus low
pressure turbine, H & W; Triple
screw; 11,900 IHP; 14, max 15 kn;
Passengers: 240 1st class, 180 2nd
class, 700 3rd class.

1913 Oct 2: Launched. Originally
intended to be named *Ormeda*.
1914 Feb: Completed.
Feb 19: Maiden voyage
Liverpool-Valparaiso.
Nov 1: First voyage from Liverpool
under charter to Cunard.
1918 Dec: The *Orduña* collided
with the Elder Dempster liner
Konakry off Galley Head. The
Konakry sank.
1919 Dec: End of Cunard charter.
1920 Liverpool-South America
West Coast.
1921 May 28: First voyage
Hamburg-New York under charter
to Royal Mail Line.
1923 Jan 1: To Royal Mail Line.
Passenger accommodation: 190 1st
class, 221 2nd class, 476 3rd class.
1926 Converted to oil-firing by
Harland & Wolff. Passenger
accommodation: 234 1st class, 186
2nd class, 458 3rd class.
1927 Back to Pacific Steam Nav
Co. Used on Liverpool-South
America West Coast service again.
1941 Feb: Troop transport.
1950 Nov: The *Orduña* returned
from her last voyage as troop
transport. Laid up.
1951 Sold to be broken up at
Dalmuir.

Steamship *Orbita*
Pacific Steam Nav Co, Liverpool

Builders: Harland & Wolff, Belfast
Yard no: 440
15,678 GRT; 173.4 × 20.5 m /
568.9 × 67 ft; III exp eng plus low
pressure turbine, H & W; Triple
screw; 11,900 IHP; 14, max 15 kn;
Passengers: 190 1st class, 221 2nd
class, 476 3rd class.

1914 Jul 7: Launched.
1915 Apr: Completed. Used as
auxiliary cruiser and troop
transport during First World War.
1919 Mar: Alterations and
overhaul by Harland & Wolff,
lasting until September 9 1919.
15,486 GRT.
Sep: Maiden voyage
Liverpool-South America West
Coast.
1921 Apr 30: First voyage
Hamburg-New York under charter
to Royal Mail Line.
1923 Jan 1: To Royal Mail Line.
1927 Converted to oil-firing by
Harland & Wolff.
Back to Pacific Steam Nav Co.
Liverpool-South America West
Coast service again.
1941 During Second World War
and the years following the *Orbita*
sailed as troop transport.
1950 Broken up at Newport, Mon.

Steamship *Orca*
Pacific Steam Nav Co, Liverpool

1927 Calgaric

Builders: Harland & Wolff, Belfast
Yard no: 442
16,063 GRT; 174.9 × 20.5 m /
574 × 67.3 ft; III exp eng plus low
pressure turbine, H & W; Triple
screw; 11,900 IHP; 14, max 15 kn;
Passengers: 190 1st class, 220 2nd
class, 480 3rd class.

1918 Jan 15: Launched.
May: Completed as cargo carrier
without passenger
accommodation. 15,120 GRT.
Transport service for the Shipping
Controller.
1921 Feb 18: The *Orca* arrived at
Belfast, where she was refitted as a
passenger ship by Harland &
Wolff.
1922 Dec: Completed.
1923 Jan 1: Sold to Royal Mail
Line.
Jan 3: Maiden voyage
Hamburg-New York.
1927 Feb: Sold to White Star Line
and renamed *Calgaric*. Passenger
accommodation altered: 290 1st
class, 550 tourist class, 330 3rd
class.
May 4: First voyage
Liverpool-Montreal.
1929 Apr 20: First voyage
London-Montreal.
1930 Sep: Laid up at Milford
Haven.
1933 Jun 9: Liverpool-Montreal
service.
Sep 9: Laid up at Milford Haven
once more.
1934 Dec 25: The *Calgaric* arrived
at Rosyth, where she was broken up
during 1935.

1

2

3

4

1 *The PSNC liner* Orduña.
2 *The* Orbita *was used as a troop transport in two World Wars.*
3 *The* Orca *was completed in 1918, provisionally as a cargo carrier.*
4 *In 1922 the* Orca *was fitted out as a passenger ship, as originally intended.*

Turbine steamer *Oropesa*
Pacific Steam Nav Co, Liverpool

Builders: Cammell Laird & Co,
Birkenhead
Yard no: 835
14,072 GRT; 168.2 × 20.2 m /
552 × 66.3 ft; Geared turbines,
Parsons; Twin screw; 10,600 SHP;
14.5 kn; Passengers: 141 1st class,
131 2nd class, 360 3rd class.

1919 Dec 9: Launched.
1920 Sep 4: Maiden voyage
Liverpool-South America West
Coast.
1921 May 14: First voyage
Hamburg-New York under charter
to Royal Mail Lines.
1923 Liverpool-Valparaiso service
again for PSNC.
1924 Converted to oil-firing.
1931 Jun 21: Laid up at
Dartmouth.
1937 Re-entered South America
service.
Troop transport during Second
World War.
1941 Jan 16: Torpedoed by the
German submarine *U 96* 100
nautical miles northwest of Bloody
Foreland (Northern Ireland). The
Oropesa sank two and a half hours
later, after the *U 96* had scored two
further torpedo hits. 113 dead.

Turbine steamer *Oroya*
Pacific Steam Nav Co, Liverpool

Builders: Harland & Wolff, Belfast
Yard no: 506
12,257 GRT; 165.1 × 19.1 m /
542 × 62.7 ft; Geared turbines,
Brown-Curtis-H & W; Twin
screw; 10,000 SHP; 14.5 kn;
Passengers: 150 1st class, 123 2nd
class, 450 3rd class.

1920 Dec 16: Launched, then
laid up before completion. PSNC
had temporarily no use for the ship
because of a recession in the trade
with Chile.
1922 Building resumed.
1923 Mar 22: Delivered.
Liverpool-Valparaiso service.
1931 Sep 8: Laid up at
Dartmouth.
1938 Dec: Sold to be broken up
1939 Feb 1: Towed by the Dutcl
tug *Rode Zee,* the *Oroya* left
Dartmouth for La Spezia.

5 *The* Oropesa *sank in 1941 after three
torpedo hits.*
6 *The* Oroya *during the seven years she
was laid up at Dartmouth.*

Patria and Providence

Steamship *Patria*
Cyprien Fabre, Marseille

Builders: F et Ch de la
Méditerranée, La Seyne
Yard no: 1058
11,885 GRT; 156.1 × 18.2 m /
512 × 59.7 ft; III exp eng from
builders; Twin screw; 11,000 IHP;
17, max 18 kn; Passengers: 140 1st
class, 250 2nd class, 1,850 3rd
class.

1913 Nov 11: Launched.
1914 Apr: Completed.
Apr 16: Maiden voyage
Marseille-New York.
1932 Jan 19: Chartered to
Messageries Maritimes. Used on
route between Marseille and
Eastern Mediterranean.
1940 Jan 1: Sold to Messageries
Maritimes.
Jun: Laid up at Haifa following the
capitulation of France.
Nov: Entered service again under
British control. The ship was
supposed to leave for Mauritius on
November 23 with 1,900 emigrants
from Palestine. The sailing date
was postponed, and the liner
waited at Haifa with the emigrants
on board.
On the morning of November 25
the *Patria* was rocked by three
explosions. The ship heeled over
and lay on the bottom in shallow
water on her starboard side, 279
people fell victim to this act of
sabotage. The perpetrators were
never found.
1952 The wreck was scrapped.

Steamship *Providence*
Cyprien Fabre, Marseille

Builders: F et Ch de la
Méditerranée, La Seyne
Yard no: 1066
11,996 GRT; 156.0 × 18.2 m /
512 × 59.7 ft; III exp eng from
builders; Twin screw; 11,000 IHP;
17, max 18 kn; Passengers: 140 1st
class, 250 2nd class, 1,850 3rd
class.

1914 Aug 4: Launched.
Laid up incomplete in building
dock for duration of First World
War.
1920 May: Completed.
Jun 1: Maiden voyage
Marseille-New York.
1932 Jan: Chartered to
Messageries Maritimes. Used on
route between Marseille and
Eastern Mediterranean.
1940 Jan 1: Sold to Messageries
Maritimes, Marseille.
June: Laid up at Berre following
the French capitulation. During a
storm the *Providence's* anchor
chains broke and she was driven
ashore.
1944 Dec 15: The ship was
salvaged. Rebuilt with passenger
accommodation for 222 1st class,
294 2nd class, 284 3rd class.
Used again on Mediterranean
service.
1951 Dec: Sold to be broken up at
La Spezia.

1 *The Cyprien Fabre liner* Patria *was
the first ship to have a cinema on
board.*

2

3

2 *The* Providence *with a black hull at the end of the '20s.*

3 *The* Providence *sailed in the Mediterranean under the flag of Messageries Maritimes.*

The Columbus-Class of North German Lloyd

Steamship *Columbus*
North German Lloyd, Bremen

1920 *Homeric*

Builders: Schichau, Danzig
Yard no: 891
34,351 GRT; 236.0 × 25.1 m /
774 × 82.3 ft; III exp eng,
Schichau; Twin screw; 32,000 IHP;
18, max 19 kn; Passengers: 529 1st
class, 487 2nd class, 1,750 3rd
class; Crew: 730.

1913 Dec 17: Launched.
1914 Aug: Following the outbreak
of war, construction was halted
on the 80 per cent completed ship.
1919 Jun 28: The Treaty of
Versailles stipulated that the
Columbus should be handed over
to Great Britain.
1920 June: The White Star Line,
Liverpool, bought the new ship and
renamed her *Homeric.* Building
continued under British
supervision.
1922 Jan 21: Arrived in
Southampton following
completion and trials.
Feb 15: Maiden voyage
Southampton-New York.
1923 Oct: Refit by Harland &
Wolff, lasting until March, 1924.
Oil-firing and improvements to
engines. 19.5 kn service speed.
1932 Jun: Used solely for cruising.
1934 Feb: White Star and Cunard
Line amalgamated to form
Cunard-White Star Ltd.
1935 Sep: Laid up.
1936 Feb: Sold for breaking-up to
T.W. Ward, Inverkeithing.

1 *Steamship* Columbus *during
construction at the Schichau yard at
Danzig.*
2 *In 1922 the* Columbus *was handed
over to the White Star Line to become
the* Homeric.

1

2

Steamship *Columbus*
North German Lloyd, Bremen

Builders: Schichau, Danzig
Yard no: 929
32,354 GRT; 236.2 × 25.3 m /
775 × 83.0 ft; III exp eng,
Schichau; Twin screw; 32,000 IHP;
18, max 19 kn; Passengers: 513 1st
class, 574 2nd class, 705 3rd class;
Crew: 733.

1914 Laid down. Double bottom
completed by outbreak of war, then
building halted until 1920.
During the war it was planned to
name the ship *Hindenburg*.
1922 Jun 17: Naming ceremony.
In the launching which followed,
the *Columbus* moved only a few
yards towards the water.
Unsuccessful attempts to launch
the ship with the assistance of a
tug.
Aug 12: Launched.
1923 Nov 27: Completed.
1924 Apr 22: Maiden voyage
Bremerhaven-New York. Cruising.
1927 Aug 2: The starboard shaft
broke in mid-Atlantic causing the
machinery to race and destroy
itself. At the Vulkan yard at
Bremen a substitute triple
expansion engine with max 6,500
IPH was transferred from the cargo
vessel *Schwaben*.
17.5 kn at 20,000 IHP.
1929 Dec 6: Trials after refit by
Blohm & Voss. Propulsion now by
geared turbines. 49,000 SHP; 22,
max 23 kn. 32,565 GRT.
1939 Aug: The *Columbus* was on a
cruise in the Caribbean. Because of
the war danger, the passengers
were landed at Havana, and the
ship subsequently sought
sanctuary at Vera Cruz.
Dec 14: The ship sailed in an
attempt to break through to
Germany. In her wake followed two
US destroyers, which were later
relieved by the US cruiser
Tuscaloosa.
Dec 19: The British destroyer
Hyperion appeared and ordered
the *Columbus* to stop. The
Germans set their ship on fire and
opened the sea cocks. The
Columbus sank 320 miles east of
Cape Hatteras. The crew were
taken on board the *Tuscaloosa*.

3

4

5

3 *The second* Columbus. *The ship was
originally intended to be named*
Hindenburg.
4 *In 1929 the* Columbus *was converted
to turbine propulsion and given lower
funnels.*
5 *The scuttling of the* Columbus. *In
the foreground is the destroyer*
Hyperion.

Turbine steamer *Admiral von Tirpitz*
Hamburg-America Line, Hamburg

1914 *Tirpitz*
1921 *Empress of China*
1922 *Empress of Australia*

Builders: 'Vulcan', Stettin
Yard no: 333
21,498 GRT; 187.4 × 22.9 m / 615 × 75.1 ft; Turbines, with Föttinger hydraulic gearing, Vulcan; Twin screw; 16.5, max 17 kn; Passengers: 370 1st class, 190 2nd class, 415 3rd class; 1,000 steerage; Crew: 500.

1913 Dec 20: Launched.
1914 Feb: Name changed to *Tirpitz*.
Aug: Work on ship halted for duration of war.
1920 Nov: Completed.
Dec 1: Handed over to Great Britain. Managed for the Shipping Controller by P & O Line. Troop transport.
1921 Jul 25: Sold to Canadian Pacific, London.
Jul 28: Re-named *Empress of China*.
Aug 20: Overhaul and alterations commenced by Vulcan, Hamburg, and J. Brown, Clydebank, which lasted until May, 1922. 21,860 GRT.
1922 Renamed *Empress of Australia*.
Jun 16: From Glasgow to Vancouver, and thence Pacific service to Yokohama.
1923 Sep 1: Rescued hundreds of people from the great Tokyo earthquake. The first shock shattered the Yokohama pier from which the ship was just putting to sea. The *Empress* was literally swirled through the harbour. She was brought under control and boats lowered. In an attempt to move astern, her screws became entangled in the anchor chains of another vessel. The *Empress* was unmanoeuvrable and collided with a Japanese cargo vessel. She was now drifting with over 2,000 people on board towards a burning oilfield. She radioed an SOS and was towed into open water by the Dutch tanker *Iris*. The liner's boats continued the rescue work.
1926 Aug: New Parsons turbines fitted by Fairfield, Glasgow, the work lasting until June, 1927. 18,000 SHP; 19 kn; max 20 kn. Passengers: 400 1st class, 150 2nd class, 630 3rd class.
1927 Jun 25: First voyage Southampton-Quebec. Cruising.
1933 Passengers: 387 1st class, 394 tourist class, 358 3rd class.
1939 Sep: The *Empress of Australia* became a troop transport and remained so after the war.
1952 May 7: Sold to British Iron & Steel Corp and broken up at Inverkeithing.

1

2

3

1 *The* Tirpitz *at the Vulcan yard at Hamburg in 1921.*
2 *Canadian Pacific liner* Empress of Australia *ex* Tirpitz.
3 *The* Empress of Australia *as a troop transport in 1945.*

Steamship *William O'Swald*
Hamburg-America Line,
Hamburg.

1920 *Brabantia*
1922 *Resolute*
1935 *Lombardia*

Builders: A.G. 'Weser', Bremen
Yard no: 193
20,200 GRT; 187.9 × 22.0 m /
616 × 72.2 ft; III exp eng plus low
pressure turbine, Weser; Triple
screw; 17,000 IHP; 16, max 17 kn;
Passengers: 335 1st class, 284 2nd
class, 469 3rd class, 857 steerage;
Crew: 450.

1914 Mar 30: Launched.
Aug: Building halted for duration
of war.
1916 Sold to Royal Holland Lloyd,
Amsterdam. For further details see
page 52 under *Johann Heinrich
Burchard.*

1920 Jul 28: Completed, having
been renamed *Brabantia.*
Amsterdam-La Plata ports service.
1922 Sold to United American
Lines. Adapted for North Atlantic
service. 19,653 GRT. Passengers:
290 1st class, 320 2nd class, 400
3rd class.
Renamed *Resolute.*
Apr 11: First voyage Hamburg-
New York. Timetable co-operation
with Hamburg-America Line.
Cruising.
1923 Registered in Panama to
evade Prohibition laws. 17,258
GRT.
1926 Aug 6: *Resolute* bought by
Hamburg-America Line. Same
service. New measurement: 19,692
GRT.
1928 Cruising exclusively.
1934 Passengers: 497 1st class.

1935 Aug 22: Sold to Italian
government as troop transport.
Managed by Lloyd Triestino,
Genoa. After refit,
accommodation for 103 1st class
passengers and 4,420 soldiers.
20,006 GRT. Renamed
Lombardia.
1943 Aug 4: Allied air raid on
Naples. The *Lombardia* was hit,
burned out and sank.
1946 The wreck was raised and
scrapped at La Spezia.

4 *In 1926 the Hamburg-America Line
bought the* Resolute, *which had been
launched as the* William O'Swald *in
1914.*
5 *From 1928 the* Resolute *was engaged
solely on cruising. The photo below
shows the wreck of the* Lombardia *at
Naples in 1946.*

4

5

Steamship *Johann Heinrich Burchard*
Hamburg-America Line, Hamburg

1920 *Limburgia*
1922 *Reliance*

Builders: Tecklenborg, Geestemünde
Yard no: 256
19,980 GRT; 187.4 × 21.9 m / 615 × 71.9 ft; III exp eng plus low pressure turbine, Tecklenborg; Triple screw; 17,000 IHP; 16, max 17 kn; Passengers: 315 1st class, 301 2nd class, 850 3rd class; Crew: 480.

1914 Feb 10: Launched.
1915 Nov 20: Completed.
1916 Jun 8: Sold to Royal Holland Lloyd, Amsterdam, for delivery at the end of the war. The reason behind this sale was a German-Dutch agreement concerning the replacement of Dutch ships sunk by Germany. The Allied powers would not recognise the transaction and after the war demanded that the *Burchard* and her sister ship *William O'Swald* be handed over. There was thus considerable delay before the Dutch took delivery.
1920 Feb 3: Renamed *Limburgia,* the ship left Bremerhaven for Amsterdam. In the fog, she was able to shake off a British destroyer which was intended to prevent the transfer.
Service Amsterdam-La Plata ports.
1922 Due to persistent arguments about the take-over and to unprofitability, the vessel was sold to United American Lines, New York. Refit. Passengers: 290 1st class, 320 2nd class, 400 3rd class. 19,582 GRT. Renamed *Reliance.* May 3: First voyage Hamburg-New York in timetable co-operation with Hamburg-America Line. At the same time, cruising.
1923 Registered under the Panama flag because of American Prohibition laws. 16,798 GRT.
1926 Jul 27: Hamburg-America Line bought the ship back, keeping her on the same service. Measurement: 19,527 GRT.
1928 Cruising exclusively. 19,802 GRT.
1934 Passengers: 500 1st class.
1937 After refit and modernisation by Blohm & Voss, 19,618 GRT. Passengers: 633 1st class, 186 2nd class.
1938 Aug 7: For reasons unknown, the *Reliance* caught fire in Hamburg harbour and was abandoned to underwriters as a total loss. The wreck was laid up at Hamburg.
1940 Jan 4: Sold to Krupp to be broken up.
1941 Broken up at Bremerhaven.

6

7

8

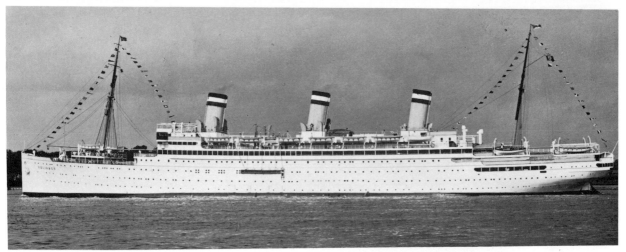

9

6 *The* Limburgia *ex* Johann Heinrich
Burchard.
7 *United American liner* Reliance.
8 *In 1926 the* Reliance *came under
the Hamburg-America Line flag.*
9 *The end of the* Reliance.

Like the emigrant ships described on pages 167-171 of Volume I, the following five steamers are not strictly applicable here. Taking into account their often unused steerage passenger capacity without cabin facilities, which affects their definition as passenger ships, they must be regarded as borderline cases.

Steamship *Hororata*
New Zealand Line, Plymouth

1939 *Waroonga*

Builders: Denny, Dumbarton
Yard no: 993
11,243 GRT; 161.5 × 20.1 m / 530 × 65.9 ft; IV exp eng, Denny; Twin screw; 6,000 IHP; 14 kn; Passengers: steerage.

1913 Dec 29: Launched.

1914 Completed. Great Britain-New Zealand service. Troop transport during First World War.
1939 May: Sold to British India Line. 9,365 GRT. Renamed *Waroonga*.
1943 Apr 5: During a voyage in convoy from New York to Liverpool, the *Waroonga* was torpedoed and sunk by the German submarine *U 635* in position 57° 10′N-35° 14′W.

Steamship *Tyndareus*
Blue Funnel Line, Liverpool

Builders: Scott's, Greenock
Yard no: 460
11,347 GRT; 157.9 × 19.8 m / 518 × 65.0 ft; III exp eng, Scott's; Twin screw; 6,000 IHP; 14 kn; Passengers: steerage.

1915 Dec: Launched.
1916 Completed. Entered service as troop transport.
After First World War, in trans-Pacific service.
After Second World War, Glasgow-Australia service.
1950 Pilgrim voyages, Indonesia-Jeddah.
1960 Sep 9: Arrived at Hong Kong to be broken up.

1 *New Zealand liner* Hororata.

2

3

2 *The* Tyndareus, *Blue Funnel Line.*
3 *On February 6 1917, the* Tyndareus
*was saved with some difficulty after
striking a mine off Cape Agulhas.*

Turbine steamer *Achilles*
Blue Funnel Line, Liverpool

1940 Blenheim

Builders: Scott's, Greenock
Yard no: 481
11,426 GRT; 157.9 × 19.8 m /
518 × 65.0 ft; Geared turbines,
Scott's; Twin screw; 7,000 SHP; 14
kn; Passengers: steerage.

1920 Jan 8: Launched.
Jun 4: Completed. Trans-Pacific
service Far East-USA.
1940 Aug: Sold to British
Admiralty. Refitted as
destroyer-depotship. Renamed
Blenheim.
1948 Broken up at Barrow.

Turbine steamer *Philoctetes*
Blue Funnel Line, Liverpool

Builders: Scott's, Greenock
Yard no: 505
11,446 GRT; 161.3 × 19.8 m /
529 × 65 ft; Geared turbines,
Scott's; Twin screw; 7,000 SHP; 14
kn; Passengers: steerage.

1922 May 25: Launched.
Aug: Completed.
Trans-Pacific service, Far
East-USA.
1940 Aug: Sold to the British
Admiralty. Refitted as
destroyer-depotship.
1948 Broken up at Newport, Mon.

Turbine steamer *Mahana*
Shaw, Savill & Albion,
Southampton

Builders: Workman, Clark & Co,
Belfast
Yard no: 349
11,796 GRT; 158.7 × 20.1 m /
521 × 65.9 ft; Geared turbines,
Parsons; Twin screw; 6,000 SHP,
13, max 14 kn; Passengers:
steerage.

1917 Jan 11: Launched.
Jul: Completed.
Southampton-Wellington service.
Measurement as shelter decker:
8,740 GRT.
1953 Broken up at Dalmuir.

4 Achilles (*photo*) *and* Philoctetes *were Blue Funnel Line's first turbine steamers.*
5 *The* Mahana *was employed on service to New Zealand.*

4

5

Porthos, Sphinx and Athos

Steamship *Porthos*
Messageries Maritimes, Marseille

Builders: Ch et A de la Gironde,
Bordeaux
Yard no: 153
12,633 GRT; 160.9 × 18.7 m /
528 × 61.3 ft; III exp eng,
Schneider; Twin screw; 9,000 IHP;
15, max 17.5 kn; Passengers: 112
1st class, 96 2nd class, 90 3rd class,
1,300 steerage as necessary; Crew:
250.

1914 Jan 25: Floated in building
dock.
1915 Completed. Marseille-Far
East service.
1940 Laid up at Casablanca.
1942 Nov 8: During the Allied
landing at Casablanca the *Porthos*
was hit by bombs and rolled over
onto her side.
1945 May: The wreck was raised.
Scrapped.

Steamship *Sphinx*
Messageries Maritimes, Marseille

1940 *Subiaco*

Builders: A et Ch de la Loire, St
Nazaire
Yard no: 215
11,375 GRT; 153.3 × 18.5 m /
503 × 60.7 ft; III exp eng from
builders; Twin screw; 9,000 IHP;
15, max 17 kn; Passengers: 188 1st
class, 90 2nd class, 106 3rd class;
Crew: 250.

1914 Mar 12: Launched.
1915 Sep 23: Completed as
hospital ship for the French navy.
1918 May: Returned to
Messageries Maritimes. Used in
Marseille-Far East service.
1939 Hospital ship in French navy.
1940 Jun: Captured by the Italians
at Marseille. Renamed *Subiaco*.
1942 Sunk in Allied air raid on
Genoa.
Wreck scrapped after the war.

Steamship *Athos*
Messageries Maritimes, Marseille

Builders: A et Ch de France,
Dunkirk
12,692 GRT; 161.0 × 18.7 m /
528 × 61.4 ft; III exp eng from
builders; Twin screw; 9,000 IHP;
15, max 17.5 kn; Passengers: 112
1st class, 96 2nd class, 90 3rd class,
1,300 steerage as necessary; Crew:
250.

1914 Jul 25: Launched.
1915 Completed. Marseille-Far
East service.
1917 Feb 17: On the return voyage
to Marseille the *Athos* was
torpedoed and sunk by the German
submarine *U 65* 200 nautical miles
southwest of Malta.

1 *Messageries Maritimes liner*
Porthos, *used in the Far East service.*
Her sister ship, Athos, *fell victim to a*
German submarine in 1917.
2 *The* Sphinx, *the somewhat smaller*
half-sister to Athos *and* Porthos.
3 *The* Sphinx *in the harbour entrance*
at La Ciotat.

Steamship *Euripides*
Aberdeen Line, Aberdeen

1932 Akaroa

Builders: Harland & Wolff, Belfast
Yard no: 439
14,947 GRT; 173.6 × 20.5 m /
570 × 67.3 ft; III exp eng plus low
pressure turbine; H & W; Triple
screw; 8,300 IHP; 15 kn;
Passengers: 140 1st class, 334 3rd
class, 750 steerage as necessary.

1914 Jan 29: Launched.
Jun 6: Completed.
Jul 1: Maiden voyage
London-Brisbane.
Aug: Entered service at Brisbane as
troop transport.
1919 Feb: Australia service,
repatriation of Australian troops.
1920 Sep 25: London-Brisbane
service.
1929 Nov: London-Brisbane
service under White Star Line
management.
1932 Sold to Shaw, Savill &
Albion, Southampton. Renamed
Akaroa.
Converted to oil-firing by
Hawthorn, Leslie & Co, Newcastle.
Passengers: 200 cabin class. 15,128
GRT.
Dec 30: First voyage
Southampton-Wellington.
1946 Refitted and modernised at
Newcastle. 15,320 GRT.
190 cabin class passengers.
1954 May: Sold to be broken up at
Antwerp.

1/2 *The* Euripides *in Aberdeen Line colours (1), and as Shaw, Savill & Albion liner* Akaroa.

Transylvania and Tuscania

Turbine steamer *Transylvania*
Cunard Line, Liverpool

Builders: Scott's, Greenock
Yard no: 451
14,315 GRT; 172.8 × 20.2 m /
567 × 66.3 ft; Geared turbines,
Scott's; Twin screw; 10,000 SHP;
16 kn; Passengers: 305 1st class;
216 2nd class, 1,858 3rd class;
Crew: 350.

1914 May 23: Launched. The ship
was ordered by Cunard Line for a
joint Mediterranean-New York
service with Anchor Line.
Oct: Completed. The *Transylvania*
was the first North Atlantic liner
with geared turbines.
Nov 7: Maiden voyage
Liverpool-New York.
1915 Feb 4: Sold to Anchor Line.
Mar 26: First voyage Glasgow-New
York.
May: Troop transport.
1917 May 4: The *Transylvania* was
torpedoed and sunk by the German
submarine *U 63* two and a half
nautical miles south of Cape Vado
in the Gulf of Genoa. 413 dead.

Turbine steamer *Tuscania*
Anchor Line, Glasgow

Builders: Stephen, Glasgow
Yard no: 459
14,348 GRT; 172.8 × 20.1 m /
576 × 65.9 ft; Geared turbines,
Stephen; Twin screw; 10,000 SHP;
16 kn; Passengers: 270 1st class,
250 2nd class, 1,900 3rd class;
Crew: 350.

1914 Sep 3: Launched.
1915 Feb 2: Delivered.
Feb 6: Maiden voyage
Glasgow-New York. Originally the
Tuscania, like her sister ship, had
been intended for the joint
Mediterranean-New York service
with Cunard Line.
1915 Sep: The *Tuscania* took on
board 409 people from the burning
Greek emigrant ship *Athinai,*
adrift in the Atlantic.
1918 Feb 5: While serving as troop
transport, the *Tuscania* was
torpedoed and sunk by the German
submarine *UB 77* seven nautical
miles north of Rathlin Light. 166
dead.

1 *The* Transylvania *was the first North Atlantic liner with geared turbines.*
2 *The* Tuscania, *like her sister ship, fell victim to the submarine war.*

Two Newly-built Ships for CGT

Steamship *Lafayette*
CGT, St Nazaire

Launched as *Ile de Cuba*
1928 *Mexique*

Builders: Ch et A de Provence, Port de Bouc
Yard no: 77
11,953 GRT; 171.6 × 19.5 m / 563 × 64.0 ft; III exp eng, Provence, plus low pressure turbine, Atlantique; Quadruple screw; 14,400 IHP; 18, max 18.9 kn; Passengers: 336 1st class, 110 2nd class, 90 3rd class, 714 steerage.

1914 May 27: Launched as *Ile de Cuba* for the CGT West India service. After the decision to use the ship for the New York service, she was renamed *Lafayette*.
1915 Oct: Completed.
Nov 3: Maiden voyage Bordeaux-New York.
1916 Fitted out as hospital ship.

1919 Jul: Returned to CGT. Refitted as passenger ship. 12,220 GRT.
Nov 8: First voyage Le Havre-New York.
1924 St Nazaire-Central America service.
1928 Renamed *Mexique*.
Jan 21: First voyage St Nazaire-Vera Cruz.
1933 Converted to oil-firing by Ch et A de la Gironde, Bordeaux. Used occasionally in New York and Casablanca service during 1934/35.
1939 Jun: Laid up, intended to be broken up.
Jul: Entered service again for the transfer of Jewish refugees to Mexico.
1940 Apr: Troop transport.
Jun 19: The *Mexique* struck a magnetic mine off Le Verdon and sank.

1 *Steamship* Lafayette *as a hospital ship during the First World War.*
2 *The* Mexique, *ex* Lafayette *sailed in the CGT St Nazaire-Vera Cruz service from 1928 onwards.*

Turbine steamer *Paris*
CGT, Le Havre

Builders: Penhoët, St Nazaire
Yard no: 68
34,569 GRT; 233.0 × 26.0 m /
764 × 85.3 ft; Turbines,
Parsons-Penhoët; Quadruple
screw; 46,000 SHP; 21, max 22.44
kn; Passengers: 563 1st class, 460
2nd class, 1,092 3rd class; Crew:
648.

1913 Laid down. Building halted
at the outbreak of war in 1914, but
in 1916 it was decided to launch
the ship in order to free the slipways
for more urgent work.
1916 Sep 12: Launched.
Subsequently towed to Quiberon
and laid up, incomplete, for the
duration of the war.
1921 Jun 5: Completed.
Jun 15: Maiden voyage Le
Havre-New York.
1929 Aug: Passenger
accommodation almost completely
destroyed by an extensive fire.
Following repairs lasting five
months, the passenger
accommodation became 560 1st
class, 530 2nd class, 844 3rd class.
1939 Apr 19: The *Paris* caught fire
at her Le Havre berth and heeled
over on April 20.
1947 The wreck scrapped.

5

3/4 *GCT liner* Paris.
5 *The capsized wreck of the* Paris *at Le
Havre.*

The Zeppelin

Steamship *Zeppelin*
North German Lloyd, Bremen

1920 *Ormuz*
1927 *Dresden*

Builders: Bremer Vulkan,
Vegesack
Yard no: 579
14,167 GRT; 173.7 × 20.5 m /
570 × 67.3 ft; IV exp eng, Vulkan;
Twin screw; 9,500 IHP; 15.5 kn;
Passengers: 319 1st class, 156 2nd
class, 342 3rd class, 1,348 steerage;
Crew: 320.

1914 Jun 9: Launched.
1915 Jan 21: Completed. Laid up
for duration of war.
1919 Mar 28: Handed over to
Great Britain, and managed for the
Shipping Controller by White Star
Line.

1920 Sold to Orient SN Co,
London. Renamed *Ormuz*.
Refitted at Belfast and Rotterdam.
14,588 GRT. Passengers: 293 1st
class, 882 3rd class.
1921 Nov 12: First voyage
London-Australia.
1927 Apr: Bought by North
German Lloyd. Renamed *Dresden*.
Aug 5: First voyage
Bremerhaven-New York. Cruising.
14,690 GRT. Passengers: 399
cabin class, 288 tourist class, 284
3rd class.
1934 Jun 20: During a Norwegian
cruise the *Dresden* ran aground
near Utsire and was badly holed.
The Danish steamer *Kong Haakon*
brought 1,000 passengers and part
of the crew safely ashore.
Jun 21: The *Dresden* capsized.
Four dead.
Aug: The wreck was sold to a firm
in Stavanger to be broken up.

3

3 *The wreck of the* Dresden *off Utsire.*

1

2

1 *The* Zeppelin *on her delivery voyage to Great Britain in March, 1919.*

2 *In 1927 the ship returned under the Lloyd flag as the* Dresden.

Missanabie and Metagama

Steamship *Missanabie*
Canadian Pacific, London

Builders: Barclay, Curle & Co,
Glasgow
Yard no: 510
12,469 GRT; 158.5 × 19.6 m /
520 × 64.3 ft; IV exp eng from
builders; Twin screw; 9,000 IHP;
15, max 16 kn; Passengers: 520
cabin class, 1,200 3rd class.

1914 Jun 22: Launched.
Sep: Completed.
Oct 7: Maiden voyage
Liverpool-Montreal.
1918 Sep 9: The *Missanabie* was
torpedoed and sunk by the German
submarine *UB 87* off Cobh,
Ireland, 52 nautical miles
south-east of Daunts Rock. 45
dead.

Steamship *Metagama*
Canadian Pacific, London

Builders: Barclay, Curle & Co,
Glasgow
Yard no: 511
12,420 GRT; 158.5 × 19.6 m /
520 × 64.3 ft; IV exp eng from
builders; Twin screw; 9,000 IHP;
15, max 16 kn; Passengers: 516
cabin class, 1,138 3rd class.

1914 Nov 19: Launched.
1915 Mar: Completed.
Mar 26: Maiden voyage
Liverpool-St John.
1922 Mar 9: First voyage
Glasgow-St John.
1927 Mar 1: First voyage
Antwerp-St John.
1930 Laid up off Southend.
1934 Apr 3: Sold to P. & W.
McLellan, Bo'ness, to be broken
up.

1 *The* Missanabie, *which was sunk in 1918.*
2 *Canadian Pacific liner* Metagama.

Steamship *Kaisar-I-Hind*
P & O Line, Greenock

1921 *Emperor of India*
1921 *Kaisar-I-Hind*

Builders: Caird, Greenock
Yard no: 327
11,430 GRT; 164.6 × 18.6 m /
540 × 61.0 ft; IV exp eng, Caird;
Twin screw; 16,000 IHP; 17, max
19 kn; Passengers: 315 1st class,
233 2nd class; Crew: 367.

1914 June 28: Launched.
Oct: Completed.
Oct 24: Maiden voyage
London-Bombay.
1916 Jun: A few London-Sydney
voyages, then service as troop
transport.
1919 London-Bombay service
again.
1921 Jun 8: First voyage
Southampton-New York under
charter to Cunard, and bearing the
name *Emperor of India*.
London-Bombay service again at
end of year. Renamed *Kaisar-I-Hind*.
1926 11,518 GRT.
1938 Broken up at Blyth.

Steamship *Naldera*
P & O Line, Greenock

Builders: Caird, Greenock
Yard no: 330
15,825 GRT; 184.4 × 20.5 m /
605 × 67.3 ft; IV exp eng, Caird;
Twin screw; 18,000 IHP; 17, max
18.5 kn; Passengers: 426 1st class,
247 2nd class; Crew: 462.

1914 Laid down. Building halted
on outbreak of war. Resumed in
1917 because of British tonnage
losses. Planned for completion as
armed merchant cruiser, cargo
carrier, hospital ship, troop
transport and finally as an aircraft
carrier, but none fulfilled.
1917 Dec 29: Launched.
1920 Mar 24: Completed.
Apr 10: Maiden voyage
London-Sydney.
1931 London-Bombay-Far East
service.
1938 Laid up.
Nov: Sold to P. & W. McLellan to
be broken up and scrapped at
Bo'ness.

Steamship *Narkunda*
P & O Line, Belfast

Builders: Harland & Wolff, Belfast
Yard no: 471
16,118 GRT; 184.7 × 21.4 m /
606 × 70.2 ft; IV exp eng, H & W;
Twin screw; 18,000 IHP; 17, max
18.5 kn; Passengers: 426 1st class,
247 2nd class; Crew: 462.

1914 Laid down. Building halted
following outbreak of war, but
continued in 1917 under
circumstances similar to those of
sister ship *Naldera*.
1918 Apr 25: Launched.
1920 Mar 30: Completed.
Apr 24: Maiden voyage
London-Bombay.
Jul 9: First voyage London-Sydney.
1922 Tonnage 16,227 GRT.
1938 Converted to oil-firing.
1940 May: Troop transport.
1942 Nov 14: The *Narkunda* was
sunk by bombers off Bougie, North
Africa, while serving as transport
in the Allied invasion fleet. She had
already on November 13 been
torpedoed by the Italian submarine
Platino. 31 dead.

1

2

3

1 *The* Kaisar-I-Hind.
2 *P & O liner* Naldera.
3 *The* Narkunda *was sunk in 1942
while serving as an Allied troop
transport.*

Steamship *Statendam*
Holland-America Line,
Rotterdam

1917 Justicia

Builders: Harland & Wolff, Belfast
Yard no: 436
32,234 GRT; 236.5 × 26.3 m /
776 × 86.3 ft; III exp eng plus
low pressure turbine, H & W;
Triple screw; 22,000 IHP; 18 kn;
Passengers: 3,430 in three classes
intended; Crew: 600.

1914 Jul 9: Launched. Building
halted after outbreak of First
World War.
1917 Requisitioned by British
Government for completion as
troop transport.
Apr 7: Entered service as *Justicia*,
managed by White Star Line.
1918 Jul 19: While on a voyage
from Belfast to New York, the
Justicia was attacked by the
German submarine *UB 64* in the
North Channel, 20 nautical miles
off Skerryvore. The first torpedo
struck at 13.50, and was followed
by two more at 16.00. Tugs tried to
tow the badly damaged ship to
Lough Swilly. At 19.18 the
Justicia received another torpedo
from the *UB 64*, but remained
afloat. The *UB 64* had to break off
the attack as she was damaged
herself.
Jul 20: At 9.10 the German
submarine *UB 124* sealed the fate of
the *Justicia* with two torpedo hits.
The *Justicia* sank three hours later.
Ten dead.
The *UB 124* was damaged by depth
charges and had to surface. The
British destroyers *Marne*,
Milbrook, *Pigeon* and other vessels
sank the submarine with gunfire.

1 *The* Justicia *was launched in 1914 as
the* Statendam, *and entered service as
British troop transport in 1917.*

Steamship *Belgenland*
Red Star Line, Antwerp

1917 *Belgic*
1923 *Belgenland*
1935 *Columbia*

Builders: Harland & Wolff, Belfast
Yard no: 391
27,132 GRT; 212.3 × 23.9 m /
697 × 78.9 ft; III exp eng plus low
pressure turbine, H & W; Triple
screw; 18,500 IHP; 17, max 18 kn;
Passengers: 500 1st class, 600 2nd
class, 1,500 3rd class.

1914 Dec 31: Launched, then laid
up incomplete.
1917 The British Government
decided to have the ship completed
as a cargo carrier.
Jun 21: Delivered to White Star
Line, Liverpool as *Belgic*.
Liverpool-New York service.

24,547 GRT.
1918 Fitted out as transport at
New York, with accommodation
for approximately 3,000 troops.
1921 Apr: Laid up at Liverpool, as
no shipyard had a berth free at
which the vessel could be fitted out
in accordance with the original
plans for her completion as a
passenger liner.
1922 Mar: The *Belgic* went to the
Harland & Wolff yard at Belfast.
Refitted as passenger ship and
converted to oil-firing.
1923 Mar 17: Completed as
Belgenland for Red Star Line.
Liverpool remained the ship's
home port.
Apr 4: Maiden voyage
Antwerp-New York. Often
employed on cruising.
1933 Mar: Laid up at Antwerp.

Jul: Three Mediterranean cruises.
Sep: Laid up at London.
1935 Jan: Sold to Atlantic
Transport Co, of West Virginia,
New York. Renamed *Columbia*.
White hull. 24,578 GRT. Used in
Panama Pacific Line's New
York-California service. Taken off
as unprofitable after a few months.
An attempt to use the *Columbia* for
New York-West Indies cruises was
given up for the same reason after a
short time.
1936 Apr 22: Last voyage New
York-Bo'ness, where the ship
arrived on May 4 to be broken up
by P. & W. McLellan.

2

2 The Belgic *was launched in 1914 as
the* Belgenland. *In 1917 the ship was
completed as a cargo carrier.*

3

4

3 *The* Belgic *sailed as a cargo vessel until 1921.*
4 *In 1923 the* Belgenland *was finally refitted as a passenger ship, as had originally been planned.*

Steamship *Jan Pieterszoon Coen*
Stoomv Mij 'Nederland',
Amsterdam

Builders: Nederlandsche Sb Mij,
Amsterdam
Yard no: 130
11,692 GRT; 159.0 × 18.4 m/
522 × 60.4 ft; III exp eng, N.F.v
Werkt en Spoorw; Twin screw;
7,400 IHP; 14.5 kn; Passengers:
200 1st class, 166 2nd class, 46 3rd
class; Crew: 230.

1914 Sep 30: Launched.
1915 Jun: Completed.
Jul: Maiden voyage
Amsterdam-Dutch Indies.
1927 11,140 GRT.
1940 May 14: Sunk between the
pierheads at Ijmuiden as a
blockship.
Scrapped by 1945.

1 *Nederland liner* Jan Pieterszoon
Coen.

1

Steamship *Johan de Witt*
Stoomv Mij 'Nederland',
Amsterdam

1949 *Neptunia*

Builders: Nederlandsche Sb Mij,
Amsterdam
Yard no: 150
10,355 GRT; 152.1 × 18.1 m /
499 × 59.4 ft; III exp eng,
Werkspoor; Twin screw; 7,000
IHP; 15, max 15.5 kn; Passengers:
197 1st class, 120 2nd class, 36 3rd
class; Crew: 225.

1919 May 2: Launched.
1920 Jul 27: Completed.
Amsterdam-Dutch Indies service.
1930 Dec: Laid up.
1932 Nov: Re-entered service as
replacement for the burnt out
Pieter Corneliszoon Hooft.

1933 Apr: Refitted at
Amsterdamsche Droogdok Mij.
New Maierform forepart. 10,474
GRT; Overall length 159.4 m /
523 ft; 16 kn.
Oct 25: First voyage after refit.
1940 Laid up in Dutch Indies for a
short time, then fitted out as troop
transport at Sydney. During the
war the *Johan de Witt* sailed
under Orient Line management.
1945 Returned to 'Nederland'.
1948 Dec 15: Sold to Greek Line.
Renamed *Neptunia*. Registered in
Panama for Cia Mar del Este, and
from 1954 for Neptunia Shipping
Co. After refit, only one funnel,
and mainmast removed. 10,519
GRT.
1949 Piraeus-New York service.

1951 Apr 8: First voyage New
York-Bremerhaven. Passengers:
39 1st class, 748 tourist class.
1955 Apr 15: First voyage
Bremerhaven-Montreal. White
hull.
1957 Nov 2: While entering Cobh
the *Neptunia* struck Daunt's Rock
and was beached, badly damaged.
The ship was abandoned to
underwriters and sold to be broken
up.
1958 Mar 2: After provisional
sealing of the hull, the *Neptunia*
was towed to Hendrik Ido Ambacht
by the Dutch tug *Gele Zee* and
broken up by Simons
Scheepssloperij.

2

3

4

5

2 *The* Johan de Witt *entered service in 1920.*
3 Johan de Witt *as troop transport during the Second World War.*
4 *The* Neptunia, *ex* Johan de Witt.
5 *Greek liner* Neptunia *at Hamburg in 1956.*

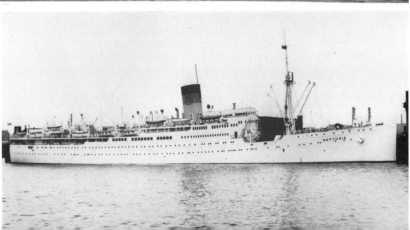

Turbine steamer *Ausonia*
Soc Ital di Servizi Marittimi,
Genoa

Builders: Blohm & Voss, Hamburg
Yard no: 236
11,300 GRT; 158.0 × 18.7 m /
518 × 61.4 ft; Geared turbines, B
& V; Twin screw; 18,000 SHP; 20
kn; Passengers: 164 1st class, 116
2nd class, 140 3rd class; Crew: 275.

1915 Apr 15: Launched, then
laid up incomplete for the duration
of the war.
1919 First negotiations between
builders and owners about a new
contract for the ship's completion.
The price estimate made by Blohm
& Voss was accepted, and the
shipowners bought the amount of
marks due at the settling of the
contract. The fall in the value of
German currency forced the
builders to revise their estimate
even before the contract was
signed. The Italians, after long
negotiations, agreed to accept the
higher price. When the builders

were then forced to ask a higher
price for the third time, because of
the worsening of inflation, the
shipowners cancelled their order
for the *Ausonia*.
1920 Negotiations between
builders and shipping line broken
off.
1922 Blohm & Voss sold the hull of
the *Ausonia* to be broken up.
Like her Italian-built sister ship
Esperia, the *Ausonia* was to have
been used in the eastern
Mediterranean.

Turbine steamer *Esperia*
Soc Ital di Servizi Marittimi,
Naples

Builders: Soc Ersercicio Bacini,
Riva Trigoso
Yard no: 66
11,398 GRT; 161.0 × 18.8 m /
528 × 61.7 ft; Geared turbines, N.
Odero; Twin screw; 19,680 SHP;
18, max 21.4 kn; Passengers: 205
1st class, 118 2nd class, 56 3rd
class, 100 steerage; Crew: 275.

1918 Launched.
1921 Completed.
Mar: Maiden voyage
Genoa-Alexandria-Venice.
1932 To Lloyd Triestino, Genoa.
Genoa-Alexandria service,
occasionally extended to
Alexandria-Trieste.
1937 To 'Adriatica' SAN, Genoa.
Same route.
1941 Aug 20: While sailing in a
reinforcement convoy from Italy to
North Africa, the *Esperia* was sunk
by three torpedoes from the British
submarine *Unique*. 31 dead.

1 *The only known photograph of the
never completed* Ausonia.

2

3

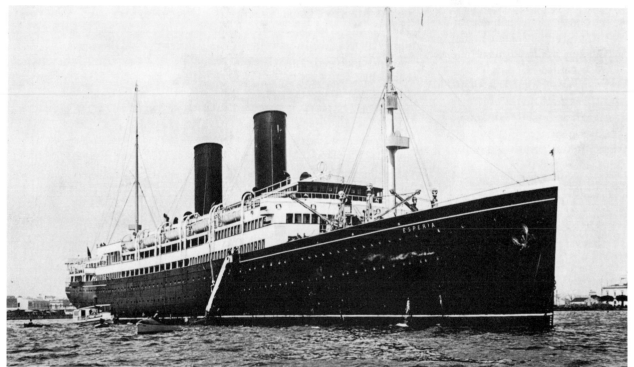

4

2 *The* Esperia *during her first years of service.*
3 *The* Esperia about 1930.
4 *The* Esperia *received her white hull while in Lloyd Triestino service.*

Steamship *San Gennaro*
'Sicula Americana'

1921 *Colombo*

Builders: Palmers, Jarrow
Yard no: 843
10,917 GRT; 163.4 × 19.5 m /
536 × 64.0 ft; IV exp eng,
Palmers; Twin screw; 10,500 IHP;
16, max 17 kn; Passengers: 2,000
in three classes planned.

1915 Oct: Launched. Laid up
incomplete because of the war.
1917 Oct: Completed as cargo
carrier. 'Sicula Americana', for
whose North Atlantic service the
ship was originally intended, had
been taken over in the meantime by
'Transoceanica', Genoa. This
company was founded on August
19 1917 as a subsidiary of
Navigazione Generale Italiana.
The *San Gennaro* sailed as a cargo
carrier for the British Shipping
Controller until 1919.
1921 Aug 20: Navigazione
Generale Italiana took over the
'Transoceanica' fleet. *San
Gennaro* was renamed *Colombo*.
Passenger accommodation: 100 1st
class, 700 2nd class and 2,000 3rd
class. 11,762 GRT.
Nov 23: First voyage Naples-New
York.
1924 12,087 GRT.
1928 Genoa-Panama-Valparaiso
service.
1932 To 'Italia' Flotta Riunite,
Genoa. Continued in South
America service.
1935 Troop transport to Massawa.
1937 To Lloyd Triestino, Genoa.
11,760 GRT.
Genoa-Massawa-Djibouti service.
1940 Jan 21: The *Colombo* rescued
survivors from the Italian liner
Orazio which had caught fire off
Marseille.
1941 Apr 8: When the Italian
naval port of Massawa, Eritrea,
was taken by British forces, the
Colombo was blown up by her
crew.
After the war the British raised the
wreck, which was scrapped in
1949.

5 *The NGI* Colombo *was launched in
1915 as the* San Gennaro.
6 *In 1937 the* Colombo *was taken over
by Lloyd Triestino.*

5

6

Turbine steamer *Aotearoa*
Union SS Co of New Zealand,
London

1916 *Avenger*

Builders: Fairfield, Glasgow
14,744 GRT; 167.6 × 20.1 m /
550 × 65.9 ft; Geared turbines,
Fairfield; Twin screw; 16,000 SHP;
18 kn; Passengers: about 600 in
three classes intended.

1915 Jun 30: Launched. She had
been laid down in 1913, but work
was halted following the outbreak
of war in 1914. On June 21 1915 the
British Admiralty took over the
ship and ordered her completion as
an auxiliary cruiser.
1916 Entered service in Royal
Navy as auxiliary cruiser *Avenger*.
1917 Jun 14: After a patrol voyage
the *Avenger* was torpedoed and
sunk by the German submarine *U
69* while on her way to Scapa Flow
in position 60° 20'N-3° 58'W. One
dead.

1 *The British auxiliary cruiser* Avenger *ex* Aotearoa.

Duilio and Giulio Cesare

Turbine steamer *Duilio*
Navigazione Generale Italiana,
Genoa

Builders: Ansaldo, Sestri Ponente
Yard no: 175
24,281 GRT; 193.5 × 23.2 m /
635 × 76.1 ft; Geared turbines,
Ansaldo; Quadruple screw;
22,000 SHP; 19 kn; Passengers:
280 1st class, 670 2nd class, 600 3rd
class; Crew: 480.

1916 Jan 9: Launched. Building
halted for duration of war.
1920 Building resumed.
1923 Oct: Completed.
Oct 30: Maiden voyage Genoa-New
York.
1928 Aug: First voyage Genoa-La
Plata ports.
1932 To 'Italia' Flotta Riunite,
Genoa.
1933 First voyage Genoa-Cape
Town.
1934 23,635 GRT after refit. 757
passengers in three classes.
1937 To Lloyd Triestino, Genoa.
Continued in Africa service.

1940 Laid up.
1942 Mar: *Duilio* was chartered by
the International Red Cross and
used for evacuation voyages from
East Africa. Laid up at Trieste in
the summer of that year.
1944 Jul 10: Sunk in Allied air raid
on Trieste.
1948 Raised and scrapped at
S Rocco, Trieste.

1

1 Duilio, *the first 20,000 tonner built
in Italy.*
2 *In 1932 the* Duilio *came under the
flag of the new 'Italia' Line.*
3 Duilio *in 1942, under charter to the
International Red Cross.*

2

3

Turbine steamer *Giulio Cesare*
Navigazione Generale Italiana,
Genoa

Builders: Swan, Hunter & Wigham
Richardson, Newcastle
Yard no: 967
21,848 GRT; 193.2 × 23.3 m /
634 × 76.4 ft; Geared turbines,
Wallsend Slipway; Quadruple
screw; 21,900 SHP; 19, max 20.5
kn; passengers: 243 1st class, 306
2nd class, 1,824 3rd class; Crew:
542.

1913 Dec: Laid down.
1914 Aug: Building halted
following outbreak of war.
1920 Feb 7: Launched.
1922 Mar: Completed.
May 4: Maiden voyage
Genoa-Buenos Aires.
Aug 11: First voyage Genoa-New
York.

1923 21,657 GRT.
1925 Genoa-Buenos Aires service.
1932 To 'Italia' Flotta Riunite,
Genoa.
1933 First voyage Genoa-Cape
Town.
1934 Refit. 21,782 GRT.
Passengers: 170 1st class, 170 2nd
class, 300 tourist class.
1937 To Lloyd Triestino, Genoa.
Far East service. 21,900 GRT.
1940 Laid up.
1942 Mar: *Giulio Cesare* was
chartered by the International
Red Cross and used for evacuation
voyages from East Africa. Laid up
at Trieste in the summer of that
year.
1944 Sep 11: *Guilio Cesare* heeled
over and sank after being hit
during an Allied air raid on Trieste.
1949 The wreck was raised and
scrapped.

4 *NGI liner* Giulio Cesare *during
trials.*
5 *The* Giulio Cesare *during the '30s.*
6 *The* Giulio Cesare *in Lloyd Triestino
colours.*

4

1/2 *The Orient liner* Ormonde *began her career as troop transport.*

Steamship *Regina*
Dominion Line, Liverpool

1930 *Westernland*

Builders: Harland & Wolff, Belfast
Yard no: 454
16,314 GRT; 183.1 × 20.7 m /
601 × 67.9 ft; III exp eng plus low
pressure turbine, H & W; Triple
screw; 12,000 IHP; 15 kn;
Passengers: from 1920: 631 cabin
class, 1,824 3rd class; Crew: 280.

1917 Apr 19: Launched.
1918 Dec: Provisionally completed
as transport. Only one funnel, no
passenger accommodation.
1920 Aug: To Belfast, refitted as
passenger ship by Harland &
Wolff. 16,500 GRT.
1922 Mar 16: First voyage
Liverpool-Portland.
1925 Dec: Dominion Line was
taken over by White Star Line.
Dec 12: First voyage Liverpool-New
York.
1929 To Red Star Line. Remained
under the British flag, registered
for F. Leyland, Liverpool.
Passengers: 350 cabin class, 350
tourist class, 800 3rd class.
1930 Renamed *Westernland*.
Antwerp-New York service.
1935 Bought by Red Star Line
GmbH, Hamburg. After a refit for
550 tourist class passengers, the
ship continued in the Antwerp-New
York service.
1936 Nov 8: The *Westernland*
sped to the assistance of the
Hamburg-America Line motor
vessel *Isis,* which had run into
difficulties in a storm off Lands
End. Only one cabin boy could be
rescued; the *Isis* had sunk in the
meantime with 39 men on board.
1939 Jun: Sold to
Holland-America Line,

Rotterdam. Same route.
1940 May: The *Westernland*
became the seat of the exiled Dutch
government at Falmouth.
Jul: Refitted at Liverpool as troop
transport.
1942 Nov: Sold to British
Admiralty. Sent to London for
conversion as repair-ship.
1946 Sold to C. Salvesen, Leith.
Conversion as whaler planned, but
not carried out.
1947 Jul 15: Sold to British Iron &
Steel Corp to be broken up.
Scrapped at Blyth.

1 *Dominion liner* Regina *at Liverpool in 1923.*

2 *The* Westernland *ex* Regina *during the Second World War.*

Steamship *Pittsburgh*
White Star Line, Liverpool

1926 *Pennland*

Builders: Harland & Wolff, Belfast
Yard no: 457
16,332 GRT; 182.9 × 20.7 m /
600 × 67.9 ft; III exp eng plus
low pressure turbine, H & W;
Triple screw; 12,000 IHP; 15 kn;
Passengers: 600 cabin class, 1,800
3rd class; Crew: 300.

1913 Nov: Laid down for
American Line, Liverpool.
Building halted during First World
War.
1920 Nov 11: Launched.
1922 May 25: Completed.
Jun 6: Maiden voyage
Liverpool-Boston. Later Boston
voyages from Hamburg and
Bremen.
Nov: Rescued the crew of the
sinking Italian cargo vessel *Monte
Grappa*.
1925 Jan: To Red Star Line.
Registered under British flag for F.
Leyland, Liverpool.
Jan 20: First voyage Antwerp-New
York.
1926 Feb: Renamed *Pennland*.
1935 Bought by Red Star Line
GmbH, Hamburg. Antwerp-New
York service continued after refit
for 550 tourist class passengers.
1939 Jun: Sold to
Holland-America Line,
Rotterdam. Same route.
1940 May: Chartered to British
Ministry of War Transport and
refitted as troop transport.
1941 Apr 25: Sunk by German
aircraft in Gulf of Athens.

3

4

3 *White Star liner* Pittsburgh.
4 *The* Westernland *ex* Regina
under the German flag.

Melita and Minnedosa

Steamship *Melita*
Canadian Pacific, Belfast

1935 *Liguria*

Builders: Harland & Wolff, Belfast
Building of hull subcontracted to
Barclay, Curle & Co, Glasgow
Yard no: 517
13,967 GRT; 166.4 × 20.5 m /
546 × 67.3 ft; III exp eng plus
low pressure turbine, H & W;
Triple screw; 11,000 IHP; 16, max
16.5 kn; Passengers: 550 cabin
class, 1,200 3rd class; Crew: 300.

1917 Apr 21: Launched.
Jun 2: Towed to Belfast. Building
continued by Harland & Wolff.
1918 Jan 12: Completed.
Jan 25: Maiden voyage as troop
transport.
1920 Liverpool-Canada service,
1922-27 from Antwerp.
1925 Refit by Palmers, Jarrow.
15,183 GRT.
1926 Passengers: 206 cabin class,
546 tourist class, 588 3rd class.
1932 Mostly cruising until 1934.

1934 Sep: Laid up.
1935 Apr 5: Sold to Ricuperi
Metallici, Turin, to be broken up.
Resold to Italian government.
Renamed *Liguria,* and managed as
troop transport by 'Italia' Flotta
Riunite, Genoa.
1937 Managed by Lloyd Triestino,
Genoa.
1940 Badly damaged by aerial
torpedo at Tobruk. Laid up.
1941 Jan 22: Burned out and
capsized after being hit by a bomb
at Tobruk.
1950 Raised by British salvage
team.
Aug 19: Towed from Tobruk to
Savona to be broken up.

2

1 *Canadian Pacific liner* Melita. *The* Melita *and her sister ship* Minnedosa *were ordered for the North Atlantic Pool partnership in 1913. Hamburg-America Line guaranteed to the builders that it would take over both ships in the event of the Pool being dissolved or not renewed. This proved to be the case at the end of 1913, when the Pool was broken up through the departure of Hamburg-America Line. Because of the war, the ship was not built for Hamburg-America Line. On March 12 1915 Canadian Pacific took over the building contract.*
2 *Lloyd Triestino liner* Liguria *ex* Melita.

Steamship *Minnedosa*
Canadian Pacific, London

1935 Piemonte

Builders: Harland & Wolff, Belfast. Building of hull sub-contracted to Barclay, Curle & Co, Glasgow
Yard no: 518
13,972 GRT; 166.4 × 20.5 m / 546 × 67.3 ft; III exp eng plus low pressure turbine, H & W; Triple screw; 11,000 IHP; 16, max 16.5 kn; Passenger: 550 cabin class, 1,200 3rd class; Crew: 300.

1917 Oct 17: Launched.
1918 May 2: Arrived at Belfast, building continued by Harland & Wolff.
Nov 21: Completed.
Dec 5: Maiden voyage as troop transport.

1919 Liverpool-Canada service, 1922/27 from Antwerp.
1925 Refit by Cammell Laird & Co, Birkenhead, and by Hawthorn, Leslie & Co at Hebburn. 15,186 GRT.
1926 Passengers: 206 cabin class, 545 tourist class, 590 3rd class.
1931 Jul: Laid up on the Clyde.
1935 Apr 5: Sold to Ricuperi Metallici, Turin, to be broken up. Resold to Italian government. Renamed *Piemonte*. Managed as troop transport by 'Italia' Flotta Riunite, Genoa.
1937 Managed by Lloyd Triestino, Genoa.
1942 Nov: Badly damaged by torpedo off Sicily. Laid up at Messina.
1943 Aug 15: The *Piemonte* was hit by several bombs during an Allied air raid and capsized.
1949 Wreck raised.
Jul 24: Towed from Messina to Spezia to be broken up.

3

4

5

3 *The* Minnedosa *after her*
completion as troop transport.
4 *The* Minnedosa *after the 1925 refit.*
5 *'Italia' liner* Piemonte *ex*
Minnedosa.

The Stavangerfjord

Steamship *Stavangerfjord*
Norwegian America Line,
Stavanger

Builders: Cammell Laird & Co,
Birkenhead
Yard no: 821
12,977 GRT; 168.5 × 19.6 m /
553 × 64.3 ft; IV exp eng from
builders; Twin screw; 9,500 IHP;
16 kn; Passengers: 88 1st class, 318
2nd class, 820 3rd class; Crew: 225.

1917 May 21: Launched.
1918 Apr 29: Transferred from
Birkenhead to New York, and laid
up there.

Sep 11: First voyage New
York-Oslo.
1924 Converted to oil-firing.
1931 Dec: Refit by AG 'Weser',
Bremen. Performance with
Bauer-Wach low pressure turbines
now 11,500 IHP. 18, max 18.75 kn.
Passengers: 147 cabin class, 207
tourist class, 820 3rd class. 13,156
GRT.
1932 Feb 23: Trials after refit.
1939 Dec: Laid up at Oslo.
1940 During the German
occupation of Norway the
Stavangerfjord served as
accommodation ship for the

German navy.
1945 Aug: First post-war voyage
Oslo-New York. Passengers: 122
1st class, 222 cabin class, 335
tourist class.
1956 General overhaul and
modernisation. 14,015 GRT.
1963 Sold to Shun Fung Iron
Works, Hong Kong, to be broken
up.
1964 Feb 4: Arrived at Hong
Kong.

1 *The final external appearance of the*
Stavangerfjord, *after 1956.*

1

Steamship *Minnekahda*
Atlantic Transport Line, Belfast

Builders: Harland & Wolff, Belfast
Yard no: 446
17,221 GRT; 196.9 × 20.2 m /
646 × 66.3 ft; III exp eng plus low
pressure turbine, H & W; Triple
screw; 13,600 IHP; 15, max 16.5
kn; Passengers; none until 1920.

1917 Mar 8: Launched. Ordered
in 1913. Laid down in 1914. During
the first years of the war building
was halted. Completed as cargo
carrier.
1919 Jan 18: First civilian voyage
as cargo vessel London-New York.
1920 Nov 3: To Atlantic Transport
of West Virginia, New York.
Accommodation for 2,150 3rd class
passengers built in by Bethlehem
Steel, Quincy. 17,281 GRT.
1921 Mar 31: First voyage
Hamburg-New York for American
Line.
1925 Mar 24: First voyage
London-New York for Atlantic
Transport Line.
1926 Passengers: 750 tourist class.
1931 Sep: Laid up at New York.
1936 Sold to be broken up.
Apr 14: Last voyage New
York-Dalmuir, under British flag.

1 *Originally ordered as a luxury liner,
the* Minnekahda *was completed in
1920 as an emigrant carrier for 2nd
class passengers.*

1

Lloyd Sabaudo Liners

Turbine steamer *Conte Rosso*
Lloyd Sabaudo, Genoa

1918 Argus

Builders: Beardmore, Glasgow
Yard no: 519
15,000 GRT approx; 172.2 × 20.7
m / 565 × 67.9 ft; Geared
turbines, Parsons-Beardmore;
Quadruple screw; 18, max 20.0 kn;
Passengers: intended numbers not
known.

1914 Jun: Laid down. On
completion the *Conte Rosso* was to
have entered service on the
Genoa-New York route.
1916 Oct: The British Admiralty
bought the hull and ordered
completion as an aircraft carrier.
1917 Dec 2: Launched.
1918 Sep 19: Trials as aircraft
carrier *Argus* of the Royal Navy.
Sep: Entered service.
1925/26 Rebuilt.
1937 Refitted as training ship and
tender for radio-controlled
aircraft.
1944 Dec: Accommodation ship
for Royal Navy.

1946 Dec 5: Sold to T.W. Ward to
be broken up. Scrapped at
Inverkeithing.

Turbine steamer *Conte Rosso*
Lloyd Sabaudo, Genoa

Builders: Beardmore, Glasgow
Yard no: 611
18,017 GRT; 180.1 × 22.6 m /
591 × 74.1 ft; Geared turbines,
Parsons-Beardmore; Twin screw;
22,000 SHP; 18.5, max 20 kn;
Passengers, 208 1st class, 268 2nd
class, 1,890 3rd class; Crew: 442.

1921 Jan 26: Launch planned. The
ship, however, stuck after a few
yards.
Feb 10: Launched.
1922 Feb: Completed.
Mar 29: Maiden voyage
Genoa-Buenos Aires.
May 15: First voyage Genoa-New
York.
1924 17,058 GRT.
1928 First voyage Genoa-La Plata
ports.

1932 Jan: To 'Italia' Flotta
Riunite, Genoa.
Feb 11: First voyage
Trieste-Shangai.
Later in the same year to Lloyd
Triestino, Trieste. 17,856 GRT.
Passengers: 250 1st class, 170 2nd
class, 220 3rd class.
1936 Refit. New boilers which
resulted in an increase in engine
performance to 25,000 SHP, with
20 kn cruising speed.
1940 Troop transport.
1941 May 24: During a voyage as
troop transport with 2,500 soldiers
on board, the *Conte Rosso* was
sunk by two torpedoes from the
British submarine *Upholder* 15
nautical miles east of Syracuse.
Over 800 dead. The *Conte Rosso*
was on her way to Tripoli in a
heavily protected convoy.

1 *The first* Conte Rosso *was completed
as British aircraft carrier* Argus.
2 *The Lloyd Sabaudo liner* Conte
Rosso *of 1922.*
3 *The* Conte Rosso *as a Lloyd Triestino
liner.*

1

Turbine steamer *Conte Verde*
Lloyd Sabaudo, Genoa

Builders: Beardmore, Glasgow
Yard no: 765
18,765 GRT; 170.5 × 22.6 m /
559 × 74.1 ft; Geared turbines,
Parsons-Beardmore; Twin screw;
22,000 SHP; 18.5, max 20 kn;
Passengers: 230 1st class, 290 2nd
class, 1,880 3rd class; Crew: 440.

1922 Oct 21: Launched.
1923 Apr 4: Completed.
Apr 21: Maiden voyage
Genoa-Buenos Aires.
Jun 13: First voyage Genoa-New
York.
1926 First voyage Genoa-La Plata
ports.
1932 Jan: To 'Italia' Flotta
Riunite, Genoa.
Aug 28: First voyage

Trieste-Shanghai. Later in the
same year to Lloyd Triestino,
Trieste. Passengers: 250 1st class,
170 2nd class, 220 3rd class.
1937 Sep 2: Ashore on Cape
Collinson off Hong Kong in
hurricane. Refloated with great
difficulty.
1940 Laid up at Shanghai.
1942 A few voyages as
prisoner-of-war exchange ship
between Japan and China on
charter to the Japanese
Government.
1943 Sep: After the Italian
capitulation the crew of the *Conte
Verde* sank their ship before the
Japanese could take possession of
it. Japanese salvors raised the ship,
which was taken to Japan after
temporary repairs. Refitted in
Japan as troop transport.
1944 Sunk near Maizuru in
American air raid.
1949 Jun: Wreck raised.
1951 Sold to Mitsui to be broken
up.

4 *The* Conte Verde *in 1932 as an
'Italia' liner.*
5 *In 1932 the* Conte Verde *came under
the Lloyd Triestino flag.*
6 *The wreck of the* Conte Verde *in
1949.*

4

6

5

Turbine steamer *Yorkshire*
Bibby Line, Liverpool

Builders: Harland & Wolff, Belfast
Yard no: 509
10,184 GRT; 152.2 × 17.7 m /
499 × 58.1 ft; Geared turbines, H
& W; Twin screw; 6,500 SHP; 15
kn; Passengers: 305 1st class;
Crew: 190.

1919 May 28: Launched.
1920 Sep 2: Completed.
Liverpool-Rangoon service.
1925 Collision in the Elbe with the
French steamer *Groix,* which had
to be beached.
1939 Oct 17: The *Yorkshire* was
torpedoed and sunk by the German
submarine *U 37* northwest of Cape
Finisterre in position 44° 52′N-
14° 31′W. 58 dead.

1

1 *Turbine steamer* Yorkshire *of the
Bibby Line.*

The US Shipping Board 535 ft-Class

Turbine steamer *Wenatchee*
US Shipping Board, Seattle
1922 *President Jefferson*
1941 *Henry T. Allen*
1946 *President Jefferson*

Builders: New York SB Corp,
Camden
Yard no: 240
14,174 GRT; 163.1 × 22.0 m /
535 × 72.2 ft; Geared turbines,
Westinghouse; Twin screw; 13,000
SHP; 17, max 18.5 kn; Passengers:
250 cabin class, 300 3rd class;
Crew: 203.

1919 May 24: Launched.
Originally laid down as hospital
ship *C.M. Schwab*.
1921 Mar: Completed.
Mar 12: Maiden voyage
Seattle-Yokohama for Admiral
Oriental Line.
1922 Renamed *President
Jefferson*.
1926 Sold by US Shipping Board
to American Mail Line, but
continued in the Admiral Oriental
Line's trans-Pacific service.
1941 Taken over by US Navy as
troop transport, renamed *Henry T.
Allen*.
1946 Handed over to US Maritime
Commission. Renamed *President
Jefferson*. Laid up.
1948 Broken up by Boston Metals.

Turbine steamer *Southern Cross*
US Shipping Board, Philadelphia

Launched as *Sea Girt*
1939 *Wharton*

Builders: New York SB Corp,
Camden
Yard no: 241
13,789 GRT; 163.1 × 22.0 m /
535 × 72.2 ft; Geared turbines,
Westinghouse; Twin screw; 13,000
SHP; 17, max 18.5 kn; Passengers:
250 1st class, 300 3rd class; Crew:
203.

1919 Jul 20: Launched as *Sea Girt*.
Laid down as troop transport
Manmasco.
1921 Renamed *Southern Cross*.
Sep: Completed. New York-La
Plata ports service for Munson
Line.
1926 Sold by US Shipping Board
to Munson Line, New York.
1938 Nov: Because of financial
difficulties the Munson Line sold
the ship to the US Maritime
Commission.
1939 Taken over by US Navy as
troop transport. Renamed
Wharton.
1947 Returned to US Maritime
Commission. Laid up.
1952 Broken up by Boston Metals.

Turbine steamer *American Legion*
US Shipping Board, Philadelphia

Builders: New York SB Corp,
Camden
Yard no: 242
13,737 GRT; 163.1 × 22.0 m /
535 × 72.2 ft; Geared turbines,
Westinghouse; Twin screw; 13,000
SHP; 17, max 18.5 kn; Passengers:
250 1st class, 300 3rd class; Crew:
203.

1919 Oct 11: Launched. Laid
down as troop transport *Koda*.
1921 Jul: Completed. New
York-La Plata ports service for
Munson Line.
1926 Sold by USSB to Munson
Line, New York.
1938 Oct: Because of financial
difficulties the Munson Line sold
the ship to the US Maritime
Commission.
1939 After refit, entered service as
US Army transport.
1941 Aug 22: Taken over by US
Navy as troop transport.
1946 Mar: Returned to US
Maritime Commission. Laid up.
1948 Broken up at Portland by
Zidell Co.

1

2

1 *The* Wenatchee, *first US Shipping
Board 535 ft liner, illustrated here with
the funnel markings of the Admiral
Orient Line.*
2 *The* Southern Cross. *The description
535 ft-Class for these standard
passenger ships was based on their
length of 535 ft. The definition was
adopted in order to distinguish between
this and the other class of US Shipping
Board standard passenger ship, which
was the 502 ft type.*

Turbine steamer *Hawkeye State*
US Shipping Board, Baltimore

1922 *President Pierce*
1941 *Hugh L. Scott*

Builders: Bethlehem SB Corp,
Sparrow's Point
Yard no: 4180
14,123 GRT; 163.1 × 20.0 m /
535 × 65.6 ft; Geared turbines
from builders; Twin screw; 13,200
SHP; 17, max 19 kn; Passengers:
259 1st class, 302 3rd class; Crew:
203.

1920 Apr 17: Launched.
Originally laid down as troop
transport *Berrien*.
1921 Jan 17: Completed. San
Francisco-Hawaii service for
Matson Navigation Co.
1922 San Francisco-Far East
service, managed by Pacific Mail
SS Co.
Renamed *President Pierce*.
1925 The Pacific Mail SS Co was
taken over by the Dollar Line. The
USSB sold the *President Pierce* to
the Dollar Line, San Francisco.
Continued in trans-Pacific service.
1934 12,579 GRT.
1938 The Dollar Line was taken
over by the US Government and
continued as American President
Lines.
1941 Jul 31: Entered service as US
Navy transport *Hugh L. Scott*.
1942 Nov 12: During the Allied
landing in North Africa the *Hugh
L. Scott* was torpedoed and sunk by
the German submarine *U 130* while
at the Fedala anchorage.

Turbine steamer *Keystone State*
US Shipping Board, Seattle

1922 *President McKinley*
1940 *J. Franklin Bell*

Builders: New York SB Corp,
Camden
Yard no: 253
14,127 GRT; 163.1 × 20.0 m /
535 × 65.6 ft; Geared turbines,
Bethlehem SB Corp; Twin screw;
13,200 SHP; 17, max 18.5 kn;
Passengers: 260 1st class, 300 3rd
class; Crew: 203.

1920 May 15: Launched.
1921 Jun: Completed.
Seattle-Yokohama service,
managed by Admiral Oriental
Line.
1922 Renamed *President
McKinley*.
1926 Apr: Sold by USSB to
American Mail Line, Seattle.
Continued in Admiral Oriental
Line's trans-Pacific service.
1940 Taken over by US Navy as
transport *J. Franklin Bell*.
1947 To US Maritime
Commission. Laid up.
1949 Broken up at Los Angeles.

3

4

3 *The* Hawkeye State *during trials in January 1921.*
4 *Admiral Oriental liner* Keystone State.

Turbine steamer *Bay State*
US Shipping Board, Camden

1922 *President Madison*
1939 *President Quezon*

Builders: New York SB Corp,
Camden
Yard no: 251
14,187 GRT; 163.1 × 20.0 m /
535 × 65.6 ft; Geared turbines,
Bethlehem SB Corp; Twin screw;
13,000 SHP; 17, max 19 kn;
Passengers: 260 1st class, 300 3rd
class; Crew 203.

1920 Jul 17: Launched.
Nov 10: Completed.
Seattle-Yokohama service,
managed by Admiral Oriental
Line.
1922 Renamed *President
Madison.*
1926 Sold by USSB to American
Mail Line, Seattle. Continued in
Admiral Oriental Line's
trans-Pacific service.
1933 Mar 24: Heeled over and
sank at Seattle.
Apr 13: Raised. Returned to
service in November after repairs.
1939 To Philipine Mail Line,
Manila. Renamed *President
Quezon.*
1940 Ran aground on the Riukiu
Islands.
The wreck raised and scrapped in
Japan.

Turbine steamer *Golden State*
US Shipping Board, San Francisco

1922 *President Cleveland*
1941 *Tasker H. Bliss*

Builders: Newport News SB & DD
Co
Yard no: 256
14,123 GRT; 163.1 × 20.0 m /
535 × 65.6 ft; Geared turbines
from builders; Twin screw; 13,200
SHP; 17, max 18.5 kn; Passengers:
260 1st class, 300 3rd class; Crew:
203.

1920 Jul 17: Launched.
1921 Completed. San
Francisco-Far East service,
managed by Pacific Mail SS Co.
1922 Renamed *President
Cleveland.*
1925 To Dollar Line, San
Francisco.
1938 The American Government
took over the Dollar Line and
continued it as the American
President Line.
1941 Jun: US Army transport,
renamed *Tasker H. Bliss.*
1942 US Navy transport.
Nov 12: During the Allied landing
in North Africa the *Tasker H. Bliss*
was torpedoed and sunk by the
German submarine *U 130* while at
the Fedala anchorage.

5 *The capsized* President Madison *ex*
Bay State *at Seattle in 1933.*
6 *Turbine steamer* Golden State.

Turbine steamer *Buckeye State*
US Shipping Board, Baltimore

1922 *President Taft*
1941 *Williard A. Holbrook*

Builders: Bethlehem SB Corp,
Sparrow's Point
Yard no: 4181
14,123 GRT; 163.1 × 20.0 m /
535 × 65.6 ft; Geared turbines
from builders; Twin screw; 13,200
SHP; 17, max 19 kn; Passengers:
259 1st class, 302 3rd class; Crew:
203.

1920 Launched. Laid down as
troop transport *Bertice*.
1921 Apr: Completed. San
Francisco-Far East service,
managed by Pacific Mail SS Co.
1922 Renamed *President Taft*.
Home port San Francisco.
1925 After the Pacific Mail SS Co
had been taken over by the Dollar
Line the latter bought the ship from
the USSB. Continued in
trans-Pacific service.
1934 12,562 GRT.
1938 The Dollar Line was taken
over by the US Government and
continued as the American
President Line.
1941 Sep: Entered service as US
Army transport *Williard A.
Holbrook*.
1943 Refit as hospital ship
commenced, planned as *Armin W.
Leuschner*. The project was not
realised. Equipped as troop
transport again.
1947 Handed over to US Maritime
Commission. Laid up.
1952 Broken up by Patapsco Scrap
Co.

Turbine steamer *Empire State*
US Shipping Board, San Francisco

1922 *President Wilson*
1940 *Maria Pipa*
1940 *Cabo de Hornos*

Builders: New York SB Corp,
Camden
Yard no: 254
14,127 GRT; 163.1 × 20.0 m /
535 × 65.6 ft; Geared turbines,
Bethlehem SB Corp; Twin screw;
17, max 19 kn; Passengers: 260 1st
class, 300 3rd class; Crew: 203.

1920 Aug 4: Launched.
1921 Completed. San
Francisco-Far East service,
managed by Pacific Mail SS Co.
1922 Renamed *President Wilson*.
1925 Pacific Mail SS Co taken over
by Dollar Line, which bought the
ship from the USSB.
1927 First voyage in
round-the-world service New
York-Hawaii-Far East-
Mediterranean-New York.
1934 12,597 GRT.
1938 The Dollar Line was taken
over by the US Government and
continued as the American
President Line.
1940 Sold to Ybarra y Cia, Seville.
Renamed *Maria Pipa*. Renamed
Cabo de Hornos in same year.
Barcelona-La Plata service.
1959 Broken up at Aviles by
Desguales y Salvamento del
Nervion SA.

Turbine steamer *Hoosier State*
US Shipping Board, San Francisco

1922 *President Lincoln*
1940 *Maria del Carmen*
1940 *Cabo de Buena Esperanza*

Builders: New York SB Corp,
Camden
Yard no: 256
14,187 GRT; 163.1 × 20.0 m /
535 × 65.6 ft; Geared turbines,
Bethlehem SB Corp; Twin screw;
13,200 SHP; 17, max 19 kn;
Passengers: 260 1st class, 300 3rd
class; Crew: 203.

1920 Oct 23: Launched.
1922 Sep 15: Completed. San
Francisco-Far East service,
managed by Pacific Mail SS Co.
Renamed *President Lincoln*.
1925 Pacific Mail SS Co taken over
by the Dollar Line, which bought
the *President Lincoln* from the
USSB.
1934 12,594 GRT.
1938 The Dollar Line was taken
over by the US Government and
continued as the American
President Line.
1940 Sold to Ybarra y Cia, Seville.
Renamed *Maria del Carmen*.
Name changed again in same year
to *Cabo de Buena Esperanza*.
Barcelona-La Plata service.
1958 Broken up at Barcelona.

7 *The former* Empire State *sailed
under the Spanish flag after 1940 as the*
Cabo de Hornos.
8 *The* Hoosier State *during trials.*

Turbine steamer *Silver State*
US Shipping Board, Seattle

1922 *President Jackson*
1940 *Zeilin*
1946 *President Jackson*

Builders: Newport News SB & DD Co
Yard no: 257
14,123 GRT; 163.1 × 20.0 m / 535 × 65.6 ft; Geared turbines from builders; Twin screw; 13,200 SHP; 17, max 18.5 kn; Passengers: 260 1st class, 300 3rd class; Crew: 203.

1920 Dec 11: Launched.
1921 May: Completed. Seattle-Yokohama service, managed by Admiral Oriental Line.
1922 Renamed *President Jackson*.
1926 Apr: Sold by USSB to American Mail Line, Seattle. Continued in Admiral Oriental Line's trans-Pacific service.
1940 US Navy transport, renamed *Zeilin*.
1946 To US Maritime Commission. Renamed *President Jackson*. Laid up.
1948 Broken up by American Shipbreakers, Wilmington.

Turbine steamer *Lone Star State*
US Shipping Board, Philadelphia

1922 *President Taft*
1922 *President Harding*
1940 *Ville de Bruges*

Builders: New York SB Corp, Camden
Yard no: 255
14,187 GRT; 163.1 × 20.0 m / 535 × 65.6 ft; Geared turbines, Bethlehem SB Corp; Twin screw; 13,200 SHP; 17, max 19 kn; Passengers: 320 1st class, 324 3rd class; Crew: 220.

1920 Dec 23: Launched.
1922 Mar: Completed. Mar 25: Maiden voyage New York-Bremerhaven. Managed by United States Lines. May: Renamed *President Taft*. Aug: Renamed *President Harding*.
1924 13,869 GRT. Passengers: 200 cabin class, 236 3rd class.
1929 Transferred to United States Lines, New York.
1940 Sold to Soc Maritime Anversoise, Antwerp. Renamed *Ville de Bruges*. May 14: The *Ville de Bruges* was sunk in the mouth of the Scheldt by German bombers.

9

10

11

9 *The* Silver State *with the funnel markings of the US Shipping Board.*
10 *The* President Harding, *United States Lines.*
11 *The burning* Ville de Bruges, *May 14 1940.*

Turbine steamer *Pine Tree State*
US Shipping Board, Seattle

1922 *President Grant*
1940 *Harris*
1946 *President Grant*

Builders: Bethlehem SB Corp,
Sparrow's Point
Yard no: 4195
14,119 GRT; 163.1 × 20.0 m /
535 × 65.6 ft; Geared turbines
from builders; Twin screw; 13,200
SHP; 17, max 19 kn; Passengers:
260 1st class, 300 3rd class; Crew:
203.

1921 Mar 19: Launched.
Oct: Completed.
Seattle-Yokohama service,
managed by Admiral Oriental
Line.
1922 Renamed *President Grant*.
1925 Sold by USSB to American
Mail Line, Seattle. Continued in
Admiral Oriental Line's
trans-Pacific service.
1940 Taken over by US Navy as
transport *Harris*.
1946 Handed over to US Maritime
Commission. Name reverted to
President Grant again. Laid up.
1947 Broken up at Wilmington.

Turbine steamer *Pan America*
US Shipping Board, Baltimore

Launched as *Palmetto State*
1939 *Hunter Ligget*

Builders: Bethlehem SB Corp,
Sparrow's Point
Yard no: 4196
13,712 GRT; 163.1 × 20.0 m /
535 × 65.6 ft; Geared turbines
from builders; Twin screw; 13,200
SHP; 17, max 19 kn; Passengers:
260 1st class, 300 3rd class; Crew:
203.

1921 Jun 4: Launched as
Palmetto State.
1922 Feb: Completed. Renamed
Pan America before delivery.
New York-La Plata service,
managed by Munson Line.
1926 The Munson Line, New
York, bought the *Pan America*
from the USSB.
1938 Nov: Because of the Munson
Line's financial difficulties the US
Maritime Commission took over
the company's ships.
1939 Feb: In service as US Army
transport *Hunter Ligget*.
1941 Jun: US Navy transport.
1946 Mar 18: US Army transport
again. Returned to US Maritime
Commission shortly afterwards.
Laid up.
1948 Broken up by Boston Metals.

12 *US Navy transport* Harris, *formerly the* Pine Tree State.
13 *The Munson liner* Pan America *in Hamburg harbour.*

Turbine steamer *Peninsula State*
US Shipping Board, Philadelphia

1922 *President Pierce*
1922 *President Roosevelt*
1941 *Joseph T. Dickman*

Builders: New York SB Corp,
Camden
Yard no: 252
14,187 GRT; 163.1 × 20.0 m /
535 × 65.6 ft; Geared turbines,
Bethlehem SB Corp; Twin screw;
13,200 SHP; 17, max 19 kn;
Passengers: 320 1st class, 324 2nd
class; Crew: 220.

1921 Jul 6: Launched.
1922 Jan: Completed.
Feb: Maiden voyage New
York-Bremerhaven, managed by
United States Lines.
May: Renamed *President Pierce*.
Jun: Renamed *President
Roosevelt*.
1924 13,869 GRT. Passengers:
201 cabin class, 236 3rd class.
1926 Jan: On a voyage from New
York to Bremerhaven the
President Roosevelt received a
distress call from the British cargo
vessel *Antigone*. The latter, with an
overflowing grain cargo, broken
rudder and partially flooded boiler
room, was in danger of sinking in a
snow storm. The Americans set
course for the *Antigone*. An
attempt at towing had to be given
up as even the auxiliary machinery
on the British vessel had ceased to
function. The liner lost the
Antigone in a hailstorm, and she
only came into sight again after a
search lasting seven hours. The
President Roosevelt lowered a
boat, but it was smashed to pieces
against the side when two
American seamen lost their lives. A
second boat managed to rescue 12

people from the *Antigone*. After
several unsuccessful attempts, the
last 13 *Antigone* seamen were
rescued as well. The whole rescue
action, hindered by the incessant
snowstorms, had lasted more than
four days and cost the Americans
two lives and six lifeboats.
1929 Transferred to United States
Lines, New York.
First voyage New York-Hamburg.
1940 To US Army. Refitted as
troop transport.
1941 Jun: In service as US Navy
transport *Joseph T. Dickman*.
1946 Mar: Laid up.
1947 To US Maritime
Commission.
1948 Broken up by Kaiser Co,
Oakland.

Turbine steamer *Western World*
US Shipping Board, Baltimore

Launched as *Nutmeg State*
1941 *Leonard Wood*

Builders: Bethlehem SB Corp,
Sparrow's Point
Yard no: 4197
13,712 GRT; 163.1 × 20.0 m / 535
× 65.6 ft; Geared turbines from
builders; Twin screw; 13,200 SHP;
17, max 19 kn; Passengers: 260 1st
class, 300 3rd class; Crew: 203

1912 Sep 19: Launched as *Nutmeg
State*.
1922 Renamed *Western World*.
May: Completed. New York-La
Plata service, managed by
Munson Line.
1926 Sold by USSB to Munson
Line, New York.
1931 Aug: Stranded on Boi Point
near Santos. Passengers taken off
by Hamburg-America liner
General Osorio. The *Western
World* was refloated four weeks
later.
1938 Nov: The US Maritime
Commission took over the Munson
Line's ships, the company being in
financial difficulties.
1939 In service as US Army
transport *Leonard Wood*.
1941 Jun: Taken over by US Navy
as transport.
1946 Returned to US Maritime
Commission. Laid up.
1948 Broken up by Consolidated
Builders, Vancouver, Wash.

14 *United States liner* President
Roosevelt, *formerly the* Peninsula
State. *Her dramatic rescue of the crew
of the* Antigone *caused a sensation in
1926.*

Turbine steamer *Arundel Castle*
Union-Castle Line, London

Builders: Harland & Wolff, Belfast
Yard no: 455
18,980 GRT; 201.4 × 22.0 m /
661 × 72.7 ft; Geared turbines,
H & W; Twin screw; 15,000 SHP;
17, max 18 kn; Passengers; 234 1st
class, 362 2nd class, 274 3rd class,
300 steerage; Crew: 440.

1919 Sep 11: Launched. Laid
down in 1915, with intended name
Amroth Castle.
1921 Apr 8: Completed.
Apr 22: Maiden voyage
Southampton-Cape Town.
1921 19,023 GRT.
1937 Refit by Harland & Wolff.
Forepart modernised and
lengthened, new turbines, now only
two instead of four funnels. 19,118
GRT, 209.0 m/686 ft, length
overall; service speed of 20 kn.
Passengers: 219 1st class, 167 2nd
class, 194 tourist class.
Sep 20: Trials after completion of
refit.
1939 Used as troop transport
during the Second World War.
1949 General overhaul and refit by
Harland & Wolff. Passengers: 164
1st class, 371 tourist class. 19,216
GRT.
1950 Sep: Southampton-Cape
Town service again.
1958 Dec: Last departure from
Southampton to be broken up at
Kowloon.
1959 Scrapped by Chiap Hua
Manufactory Co.

1 *Union-Castle liner* Arundel Castle.
2 *The* Arundel Castle *after her 1937
refit.*

Turbine steamer *Windsor Castle*
Union-Castle Line, London

Builders: Brown, Clydebank
Yard no: 456c
18,967 GRT; 201.4 × 22.1 m /
661 × 72.5 ft; Geared turbines,
Brown; Twin screw; 15,000 SHP;
17, max 18 kn; Passengers: 235 1st
class, 360 2nd class, 275 3rd class;
Crew: 440.

1921 Mar 9: Launched.
1922 Mar: Completed.
Apr: Maiden voyage
Southampton-Cape Town.
1937 Refitted by Harland & Wolff
in the same fashion as the sister
ship *Arundel Castle*. 19,141 GRT,
209.0 m / 686 ft, length overall; 20
kn. Passengers: 219 1st class, 191
2nd class, 194 tourist class.
1938 Jan: Southampton-Cape
Town service again after
completion of refit.
1939 Troop transport.
1943 Mar 23: While sailing in a
convoy 110 nautical miles
northwest of Algiers the *Windsor
Castle* was attacked and sunk by
German aircraft. One dead.

3 *The* Windsor Castle *at Cape Town.*
4 *The refitted* Windsor Castle *as a troop transport during the Second World War.*

Turbine steamer *Cameronia*
Anchor Line, Glasgow

1953 *Empire Clyde*

Builders: Beardmore, Glasgow
Yard no: 584
16,280 GRT; 176.3 × 21.4 m /
678 × 70.2 ft; Geared turbines
from builders; Twin screw; 13,500
SHP; 16.5, max 17 kn; Passengers:
265 1st class, 370 2nd class, 1,150
3rd class; Crew: 320.

1919 Dec 23: Launched.
1921 Mar: Completed.
May 11: Maiden voyage
Glasgow-Liverpool-New York.
1928 Nov: Refit by Beardmore.
New 60 m / 195 ft lower section to
forepart built in to counteract the
strong tendency to pitch heavily.
1929 May: Passengers: 290 cabin
class, 431 tourist class, 698 3rd
class.
1934 Dec: Laid up on the Clyde.
1935 Sep: In service as troop
transport.
1936 Jul 10: Glasgow-New York
service again.
1941 Jan: Entered service as troop
transport.
1945 Laid up at the end of the war.
1947 Entered service in spring as
troop transport to Palestine.
1948 Jul: Overhauled and refitted
as emigrant ship by Barclay, Curle
& Co. Passengers: 1,266 in one
class. 16,584 GRT.
Nov 1: First voyage
Glasgow-Sydney.
1953 Jan: Sold to Ministry of
Transport as troop transport.
Renamed *Empire Clyde*. Managed
by Anchor Line.
1957 Sep: Sold to J. Cashmore, to
be broken up.
Sep 29: Left Liverpool for Newport,
Mon.

Turbine steamer *Tyrrhenia*
Cunard Line, Liverpool

1924 *Lancastria*

Builders: Beardmore, Glasgow
Yard no: 557
16,243 GRT; 176.3 × 21.4 m /
578 × 70.2 ft; Geared turbines
from builders; Twin screw; 13,500
SHP; 16, max 17 kn; Passengers:
265 1st class, 370 2nd class, 1,150
3rd class; Crew: 320.

1920 May 31: Launched. The
Tyrrhenia had originally been
ordered for the Anchor Line as a
sister ship to the *Cameronia*.
1922 Jun 12: Delivered.
Jun 13: Maiden voyage
Glasgow-Montreal.
1923 First voyage Hamburg-New
York.
1924 New passenger
accommodation. 580 cabin class,
1,000 3rd class. Renamed
Lancastria.
1926 First voyage London-New
York.
1932 Used almost exclusively for
cruising.
1940 Mar 5: Entered service as
troop transport.
Jun 16: A day before the French
capitulation the *Lancastria*
embarked British service personnel
at St Nazaire who were being
evacuated from the path of the
advancing German troops. With
about 5,500 people on board the
ship waited at the St Nazaire
anchorage for the other ships
involved in the operation,
intending to join them in convoy for
England.
Jun 17: The *Lancastria* was
attacked by German bombers,
suffered four serious direct hits and
sank within 20 minutes.

The sinking of the *Lancastria* was
up to that time the worst
catastrophe in shipping history.
3,000 died, either in the explosions
or by drowning. 2,500 were rescued
by ships lying nearby or by vessels
which hurried out of St Nazaire.
Exact figures of the number of
victims have never been
established. The British public
only learned of the loss of the
Lancastria four weeks later, and
the number of victims was put
officially at 2,500. The 'Association
of *Lancastria* Survivors' in London
believes that more than 9,000
people were on board, of whom
only 4,000 survived.

1 *Anchor liner* Cameronia.
2 *The* Empire Clyde *ex* Cameronia.
3 *The* Lancastria *on a Norwegian
cruise. In 1940 3,000 people died when
the ship was sunk by German aircraft.*

Turbine steamer *Tuscania*
Anchor Line, Glasgow

1939 *Nea Hellas*
1955 *New York*

Builders: Fairfield, Glasgow
Yard no: 595
16,991 GRT; 176.8 × 21.4 m /
580 × 70.2 ft; Geared turbines,
Brown-Curtis-Fairfield; Twin
screw; 13,500 SHP; 16.5, max 17
kn; Passengers: 240 1st class, 377
2nd class, 1,818 3rd class; Crew:
346.

1921 Oct 4: Launched.
1922 Sep 8: Delivered.
Sep 16: Maiden voyage
Glasgow-New York.
1926 First voyage London-New
York under charter to Cunard.
1929 Passengers: 206 cabin class,
439 tourist class, 485 3rd class.
1930 Oct: Laid up until August
1931.
Often used for cruises during the
'30s. Some voyages Liverpool-India.

1939 Apr: Sold to the Greek Line,
Piraeus. Renamed *Nea Hellas*.
Passengers: 179 1st class, 404 cabin
class, 1,399 tourist class.
May 19: First voyage Piraeus-New
York.
1941 Requisitioned as troop
transport by British Ministry of
War Transport. Managed by
Anchor Line.
1947 Jan: Returned to Greek Line.
Aug: First post-war voyage
Piraeus-New York.
1954/55 Passenger
accommodation altered: 70 1st
class, 1,300 tourist class.
1955 Mar: Renamed *New York*.
Mar 24: First voyage New
York-Bremerhaven.
1959 Sep: Piraeus-New York
again.
Nov 14: Laid up at Piraeus.
1961 Oct 12: Arrived at Onomichi,
Japan, to be broken up.

Turbine steamer *California*
Anchor Line, Glasgow

Builders: Stephen, Glasgow
Yard no: 494
16,792 GRT; 176.5 × 21.3 m /
579 × 69.9 ft; Geared turbines,
Brown-Curtis-Stephen; Twin
screw; 13,500 SHP; 16 kn;
Passengers: 251 1st class, 465 2nd
class, 1,044 3rd class; Crew: 330.

1923 Apr 17: Launched.
Aug 14: Completed.
Aug 26: Maiden voyage
Glasgow-New York.
1929 Passengers: 206 cabin class,
440 tourist class, 485 3rd class.
1939 Sep: Entered service as
armed merchant cruiser.
1942 Troop transport.
1943 Jul 11: While sailing in
convoy west of Oporto, the
California was attacked by German
aircraft. The ship caught fire and
had to be abandoned. 46 dead.

4

4 *The* Tuscania *of the Anchor Line.*
5 *Greek Line liner* Nea Hellas *ex*
Tuscania. *Shown here with neutrality
markings during the first months of the
Second World War.*
6 *The* California, *last ship of the
class, was sunk by German aircraft in
1943.*

Steamship *Old North State*
US Shipping Board, Philadelphia

1922 *President van Buren*
1940 *President Fillmore*
1944 *Marigold*
1946 *President Fillmore*

Builders: New York SB Corp,
Camden
Yard no: 244
10,533 GRT; 157.3 × 19.0 m /
516 × 62.3 ft; IV exp eng from
builders; Twin screw; 6,500 IHP;
14 kn; Passengers: 78 1st class;
Crew: 117.

1920 Feb 29: Launched.
Oct: Completed.
Nov: Maiden voyage New
York-London. Managed by US
Mail Line.
1921 Aug: Managed by United
States Lines after liquidation of US
Mail Line.
1922 May: Renamed *President
van Buren.*
1923 Sep: Sold by USSB to Dollar
Line, San Francisco.
1924 First voyage in a
round-the-world-service New
York-Hawaii-Far East-
Mediterranean-New York.
1938 The Dollar Line was taken
over by the US Government and
continued as American President
Line.
1940 Renamed *President
Fillmore.*
1941 US Army transport.
1943 Oct: Refit as hospital ship
commenced, lasting until 1944.
1944 Jun: Entered service as US
Army hospital ship *Marigold.*
1946 To US Maritime
Commission. Renamed *President
Fillmore.* Laid up.
1948 Broken up at Oakland by
Kaiser Co.

Steamship *Panhandle State*
US Shipping Board, Philadelphia

1922 *President Monroe*
1940 *President Buchanan*
1944 *Emily H.M. Weder*
1946 *President Buchanan*

Builders: New York SB Corp,
Camden
Yard no: 247
10,533 GRT; 157.3 × 19.0 m /
516 × 62.3 ft; III exp eng from
builders; Twin screw; 6,500 IHP;
14 kn; Passengers: 78 1st class;
Crew: 117.

1920 Mar 9: Launched.
Aug: Completed.
Sep: Maiden voyage New
York-London. Managed by US
Mail Line.
1921 May 20: Caught fire near
Ellis Island. The cargo holds were
flooded and the ship was beached.
Refloated and repaired.
Aug: Managed by United States
Lines after liquidation of US Mail
Line.
1922 Renamed *President Monroe.*
1923 Sep: Sold by USSB to Dollar
Line, San Francisco.
1924 First voyage in round-the-
world service New York-Hawaii-
Far East-Mediterranean-New
York.
1938 The Dollar Line was taken
over by the US Government and
continued as American President
Line.
1940 Renamed *President
Buchanan.*
1943 Nov: Refit as hospital ship
commenced, which lasted until
1944, at Atlantic Basin Works.
1944 Jul: Entered service as US
Army hospital ship *Emily H.M.
Weder.*
1946 Jan: Renamed *President

Buchanan, US Army transport.
1947 To US Maritime
Commission. Laid up.
1956 Broken up by Learner Co
at San Francisco.

1 *The* Old North State *as US Mail
liner.*
2 *American President liner* President
Buchanan.

1

2

Steamship *Creole State*
US Shipping Board, San Francisco

1922 *President Hayes*
1940 *President Tyler*

Builders: New York SB Corp,
Camden
Yard no: 245
10,533 GRT; 157.3 × 19.0 m /
516 × 62.3 ft; III exp eng from
builders; Twin screw; 6,500 IHP;
14 kn; Passengers: 78 1st class;
Crew: 117.

1920 Apr 27: Launched.
Dec: Completed.
Maiden voyage New York-London.
Managed by US Mail Line. Laid up
after one voyage.
1922 Renamed *President Hayes*.
1923 First voyage in round-the-
world service New York-Hawaii-
Far East-Mediterreanean-New
York.
1938 The Dollar Line was taken
over by the US Government and
continued as American President
Line.
1940 Renamed *President Tyler*.
1941 Refit as US Army hospital
ship commenced. Planned name
Howard McCurdy. Work halted at
end of year.
1942 Jan: Entered service as US
Army transport.
1946 To US Maritime
Commission. Laid up.
1957 Mar 20: Arrived at Sun SB
Co at Philadelphia to be broken up.

Steamship *Granite State*
US Shipping Board, San Francisco

1922 *President Polk*
1940 *President Taylor*

Builders: New York SB Corp,
Camden
Yard no: 246
10,533 GRT; 157.3 × 19.0 m /
516 × 62.3 ft; III exp eng from
builders; Twin screw; 6,500 IHP;
14 kn; Passengers: 78 1st class;
Crew: 117.

1920 Jul 31: Launched.
1921 Completed.
Apr: Maiden voyage New York-
Bremerhaven. Managed by United
States Lines.
1922 Renamed *President Polk*.
Aug: First voyage New
York-London.
1923 Sep: Sold by USSB to Dollar
Line, San Francisco.
1924 First voyage in round-the-
world service New York-Hawaii-
Far East-Mediterranean-New
York.
Oct 11: Badly damaged by fire at
New York. After repairs and refit,
the island bridge was joined to the
main superstructure. 10,500 GRT.
1938 The Dollar Line was taken
over by the US Government and
continued as American President
Line.
1940 Renamed *President Taylor*.
1941 Dec: In service as US Army
transport.
1942 Feb 14: The *President
Taylor* stranded off the island of
Canton in the Pacific and had to be
abandoned. The wreck was later
destroyed by Japanese aircraft.

3

4

3 *US Army transport* President Tyler.
4 *Dollar Line's* President Polk *after
her refit in 1925.*

Steamship *Wolverine State*
US Shipping Board, San Francisco

1922 *President Harrison*
1941 *Kachidoki Maru*

Builders: New York SB Corp,
Camden
Yard no: 248
10,533 GRT; 157.3 × 19.0 m /
516 × 62.3 ft; III exp eng from
builders; Twin screw; 6,500 IHP;
14 kn; Passengers: 78 1st class;
Crew: 117.

1920 Sep 16: Launched.
1921 Jan 4: Completed. San
Francisco-Far East service,
managed by Pacific Mail SS Co
1922 Renamed *President
Harrison.*
1923 Sold by USSB to Dollar Line,
San Francisco.
1924 Jan 5: First voyage in
round-the-world service New
York-Hawaii-Far East-
Mediterranean-New York.
1930 Refit. Bridge joined to main
superstructure. 10,504 GRT.
1938 The US Government took
over the Dollar Line and continued
it as American President Line.
1941 Dec 8: The *President
Harrison* was taken by surprise at
Shanghai by the Japanese advance
and fell into their hands. Renamed
Kachidoki Maru. Placed in service
as Japanese transport.
1944 Sep 12: The *Kachidoki Maru*
was torpedoed and sunk by the US
submarine *Pampanito* 50 nautical
miles east of Hainan in position
19° 18′N-112° 23′E.

5/6 *The* Wolverine State *during trials
(5) and as* President Harrison *after the
refit of 1930.*

6

Steamship *Centennial State*
US Shipping Board, Philadelphia

1922 *President Adams*
1938 *President Grant*

Builders: New York SB Corp,
Camden
Yard no: 249
10,558 GRT; 157.3 × 19.0 m /
516 × 62.3 ft; III exp eng from
builders; Twin screw; 6,500 IHP;
14 kn; Passengers: 78 1st class;
Crew: 117.

1920 Dec 11: Launched.
1921 May: Completed.
Jun: Maiden voyage New
York-London. Managed by US
Mail Line.
Aug: Managed by United States
Lines after liquidation of US Mail
Line.
1922 May: Renamed *President
Adams*.
1923 Sep: Sold to Dollar Line, San
Francisco.
1924 First voyage in round-the-
world service New York-Hawaii-
Far East-Mediterranean-New
York.
1930 Refit. Bridge joined to main
superstructure. 10,516 GRT.
1938 The US Government took
over the Dollar Line and continued
it as American President Line.
Renamed *President Grant*.
1941 Nov: Entered service as US
Army transport.
1944 Feb 26: The *President Grant*
stranded on an underwater rock 70
nautical miles off Milne Bay, New
Guinea, and was abandoned as a
total loss.

Steamship *Blue Hen State*
US Shipping Board, Philadelphia

1922 *President Garfield*
1940 *President Madison*
1942 *Kenmore*
1942 *Refuge*
1946 *President Madison*

Builders: New York SB Corp,
Camden
Yard no: 250
10,558 GRT; 157.3 × 19.0 m /
516 × 62.3 ft; III exp eng from
builders; Twin screw; 6,500 IHP;
14 kn; Passengers: 78 1st class;
Crew: 117.

1921 Feb 23: Launched.
Jun: Completed. Maiden voyage
New York-London. Managed by
US Mail Line.
Aug: Managed by United States
Lines after liquidation of US Mail
Line.
1922 Renamed *President
Garfield*.
1923 Sep: Sold by USSB to Dollar
Line, San Francisco.
1924 First voyage in
round-the-world service New
York-Hawaii-Far East-
Mediterranean-New York.
1930 Refit. Bridge joined to main
superstructure. 10,495 GRT.
1938 The US Government took
over the Dollar Line and continued
it as American President Line.
1940 Renamed *President
Madison*.
1942 In service as US Navy
transport *Kenmore*.
1942 Converted to naval hospital
ship. Renamed *Refuge*.
1946 To US Maritime
Commission. Renamed *President
Madison*. Laid up.
1948 Broken up at Vancouver,
Wash.

7 *Steamship* Centennial State.
8 *The* Blue Hen State *during trials*.

The Scythia-Class of Cunard Line

Turbine steamer *Scythia*
Cunard Line, Liverpool

Builders: Vickers, Barrow
Yard no: 493
19,730 GRT; 190.2 × 22.4 m /
624 × 73.5 ft; Geared turbines,
Brown-Curtis-Vickers; Twin
screw; 13,500 SHP; 16 kn;
Passengers: 337 1st class, 331 2nd
class, 1,538 3rd class; Crew: 409.

1920 Mar 22: Launched.
1921 Mar: Because of strike, sent
to Lorient for final fitting out.
Aug: Completed.
Aug 20: Maiden voyage
Liverpool-New York.
1924 3rd class passenger
accommodation reduced to 1,100.
1939 Aug 27: In service as troop
transport.
1942 Nov 23: Badly damaged by
aerial torpedo at Algiers.
1943 Sep: Seaworthy again after
repairs at Gibraltar and New York.
1948 Released from service as
troop transport.
Oct: First voyage in repatriation
service Cuxhaven-Quebec/
Halifax.

1949 Nov: General overhaul and
refit commenced by Brown,
Clydebank, which lasted until
August 1950. Passengers: 248 1st
class, 630 tourist class. 19,930
GRT.
1950 Aug 17: First voyage
Liverpool-Quebec.
Sep 14: London-Quebec service.
1951 Apr 10: First voyage
Southampton-Quebec.
1958 Jan 1: Sailed from
Southampton to be broken up at
Inverkeithing.

Turbine steamer *Samaria*
Cunard Line, Liverpool

Builders: Cammell Laird & Co,
Birkenhead
Yard no: 836
19,602 GRT; 190.2 × 22.4 m /
624 × 73.5 ft; Geared turbines
from builders; Twin screw; 13,500
SHP; 16 kn; Passengers: 350 1st
class, 340 2nd class, 1,500 3rd
class; Crew: 410.

1920 Nov 27: Launched.
1921 Aug: Completed.
1922 Apr 19: Maiden voyage
Liverpool-Boston.
1924 Passenger accommodation
altered. 3rd class reduced.
1926 First voyage Liverpool-New
York.
1939 Troop transport.
1948 Sep: First voyage
Cuxhaven-Quebec/Halifax.
1950 London-Quebec service.
Autumn: Overhaul and refit by
Brown, Clydebank. 19,848 GRT.
Passengers: 248 1st class, 641
tourist class.
1951 Jun 14: First voyage
Liverpool-Quebec.
Jul 12: First voyage
Southampton-Quebec.
1956 Jan 27: Arrived at
Inverkeithing. Broken up by T.W.
Ward.

3

1 *The name ship of the class, the* Scythia, *during the '30s.*
2 The Scythia *after her 1950 refit.*
3 *Cunard liner* Samaria *as troop transport.*

Turbine steamer *Laconia*
Cunard Line, Liverpool

Builders: Swan, Hunter & Wigham Richardson, Newcastle
Yard no: 1125
19,680 GRT; 190.0 × 22.3 m / 623 × 73.2 ft; Geared turbines, Wallsend Slipway; 13,500 SHP; 16 kn; Passengers: 340 1st class, 340 2nd class, 1,500 3rd class; Crew: 410.

1921 Apr 9: Launched. The launching, originally planned for November 1920, had to be postponed because the slipway was blocked by the newly built French passenger ship *Meduana,* which had sunk after a fire.
1922 Jan: Completed.
May 25: Maiden voyage Southampton-New York, then Liverpool-New York service.
1923 Hamburg-New York service, Liverpool-New York again from 1924.
1924 Alteration and reduction of passenger accommodation. Often used for cruising during the '30s.
1939 Armed merchant cruiser in Royal Navy.
1940 Troop transport.
1942 With 2,732 people on board, including 1,800 Italian prisoners of war, the *Laconia* was sunk in the South Atlantic in position 5° 5′S-11° 38′W by two torpedoes from the German submarine *U 156.* As the submarine approached the scene of the sinking and it was realised who was on board the ship, a unique and dramatic rescue action in the history of sea warfare began. The *U 156* took on board survivors, her commanding officer called for help from all nearby ships in an open radio message and, in a coded radio message, asked assistance from the Flag-Officer of Submarines. The *U 506* and *U 507,* as well as the Italian submarine *Capellini,* were ordered to the scene of the sinking, arriving there on September 14 and 15. The Flag-Officer of Submarines, Vice-Admiral Karl Dönitz, asked the Vichy government to send rescue vessels, whereupon the French dispatched the cruiser *Gloire,* the sloop *Dumont d'Urville,* and the minesweeper *Annamite.* The German submarines were now overflowing with rescued people—Italians, Poles (who had earlier been guarding the Italians), British soldiers, and women and children. The *U 156* had at one time 260 survivors on board. A start was made to collect the *Laconia's* lifeboats together, care for the wounded and distribute provisions. On September 16 an American 'Liberator' bomber flew over the *U 156,* which had four lifeboats in tow. The submarine displayed a four square metre large Red Cross flag, and tried in vain to contact the aircraft on morse. The 'Liberator' turned away, but returned shortly afterwards and on four runs released six bombs at the *U 156,* with its unmanned guns, Red Cross flag and four boats in tow. One bomb went between the lifeboats, causing one of the boats to capsize, while another bomb exploded against the submarine, damaging it considerably. At this the *U 156* put the 55 Britons and 55 Italians still on board into the lifeboats and sailed off westwards for repairs. Despite the danger for the submarines which the incident had demonstrated, Dönitz did not call off the rescue action. Nor did he when the *U 506,* with 142 of the shipwrecked on board, was attacked by an aircraft on September 17. Fortunately the submarine was able to dive in time, so that the bombs exploded only when she was already at a depth of 60 metres/195 feet. In the course of September 17 the French ships took on the *Laconia* survivors. 1,111 people were rescued, including about 400 Italians. After completion of the rescue action, on the evening of September 17, the submarines Flag Officer issued an order to all U-boats that the rescuing of survivors from sunken ships was to be discontinued. This was decided against the background of the events which had taken place, and also because of increasing Allied aerial patrols over the Atlantic. This instruction, which became known as the 'Laconia Order', was interpreted by the British prosecutors at the Nürenberg trials as a command to murder. However, the international military court did not subscribe to this interpretation.

4 *The* Laconia. *The torpedoing of this ship gave rise to a rescue action which was unusual in time of war.*

Turbine steamer *Franconia*
Cunard Line, Liverpool

Builders: Brown, Clydebank
Yard no: 492
20,158 GRT; 190.0 × 22.3 m /
623 × 73.2 ft; Geared turbines
from builders; Twin screw; 13,500
SHP; 16 kn; Passengers: 221 1st
class, 356 2nd class, 1,266 3rd
class; Crew: 414.

1922 Oct 21: Launched.
1923 Jun: Completed.
Jun 23: Maiden voyage
Liverpool-New York. In addition
frequently employed on cruising.
1930/1931 Passenger
accommodation altered.
1939 Sep: Troop transport.
1945 Served as headquarters for
British Prime Minister Churchill at
Yalta.
1948 Aug: Released from service
as troop transport.
1949 Jun 22: First voyage
Liverpool-Quebec after overhaul
and refit.
20,341 GRT. Passengers: 253 1st
class, 600 tourist class.
1956 Dec 18: Arrived at
Inverkeithing. Broken up by T.W.
Ward.

Turbine steamer *Carinthia*
Cunard Line, Liverpool

Builders: Vickers, Barrow
Yard no: 586
20,277 GRT; 190.2 × 22.4 m /
624 × 73.5 ft; Geared turbines,
Vickers; Twin screw; 13,500 SHP;
16 kn; Passengers: 240 1st class,
460 2nd class, 950 3rd class; Crew:
450.

1925 Feb 24: Launched.
Originally to have been named
Servia.
Aug: Completed.
Aug 22: Maiden voyage
Liverpool-New York. Cruising in
addition.
1931 Passenger accommodation
altered. Cabin, tourist and 3rd
class.
1939 Sep: In service as armed
merchant cruiser.
1940 Jun 6: The *Carinthia* was
torpedoed off the Irish coast in
position 53° 13'N-10° 40'W by the
German submarine *U 46*. The
badly damaged ship remained
afloat for 30 hours before she sank
during the evening of June 7. Four
dead.

5 *Cruise liner* Franconia *during the
'30s.*
6 *The* Carinthia, *which sank in 1940
while serving as an armed merchant
cruiser.*

5

6

The Ohio ex München

Steamship *München*
Norddeutscher Lloyd, Bremen

1923 *Ohio*
1927 *Albertic*

Builders: AG 'Weser', Bremen
Yard no: 209
18,940 GRT; 187.3 × 21.8 m /
615 × 71.5 ft; IV exp eng, Weser;
Twin screw; 16,000 IHP; 17 kn;
Passengers; 229 1st class, 523 2nd
class, 690 3rd class; Crew: 400.

1914 Laid down. No building
during the war.
1919 Jun 28: Designated by the
Treaty of Versailles for handing
over to Great Britain.
1920 Mar 23: Launched.
Building resumed for Royal Mail
Line, London.
1923 Mar 26: Completed.
Mar 27: Renamed *Ohio*.
Apr 4: Maiden voyage
Hamburg-New York.
1925 Southampton-New York
service; also cruising.
1927 Feb: Sold to White Star Line,
Liverpool. Renamed *Albertic*.
Apr 22: First voyage
Liverpool-Montreal.
1928 May 5: First voyage
London-Montreal.
1929 Liverpool-New York.
1930 Liverpool-Montreal service
again.
1933 Mar: Laid up in Firth of
Clyde.
1934 Put up for sale after
amalgamation of White Star and
Cunard Line.
Jul: Sold to Japanese
shipbreakers.
Nov 29: Arrived at Osaka; broken
up there.

1 *The* München *was only completed
nine years after being laid down.
Immediately afterwards she was
renamed* Ohio.

Turbine steamer *Montcalm*
Canadian Pacific, Liverpool

1939 *Wolfe*

Builders: Brown, Clydebank
Yard no: 464
16,418 GRT; 175.3 × 21.4 m /
575 × 70.2 ft; Geared turbines,
Brown-Curtis; Twin screw; 14,000
SHP; 16, max 17.5 kn; Passengers:
542 cabin class, 1,268 3rd class;
Crew: 390.

1920 Jul 3: Launched.
1921 Dec: Completed.
1922 Jan 17: Maiden voyage
Liverpool-St John.
Apr 21: First voyage
Liverpool-Montreal.
1927 Passenger accommodation:
cabin, tourist and 3rd class.
1928 Dec 6: Fitting of new geared
turbines commenced by Harland &
Wolff. Completed the following
year.
1929 Mar 16: First voyage
Southampton-St John.
Apr 12: Antwerp-St John service.
May 14: First voyage
Hamburg-Montreal.
1932 Jul: Used almost exclusively
for cruising until 1939.
1939 Oct 17: Entered service
as armed merchant cruiser *Wolfe*.
1941 Nov: Troop transport.
1942 Jan: Conversion to
submarine depot-ship
commenced.
May 22: Sold to British Admiralty.
1943 Jan: In service as destroyer
depot-ship.
1950 Laid up as reserve ship.
1952 Nov 7: Towed to Faslane and
broken up there by Metal
Industries.

Turbine steamer *Montrose*
Canadian Pacific, Liverpool

1939 *Forfar*

Builders: Fairfield, Glasgow
Yard no: 529
16,402 GRT; 175.3 × 21.4 m /
575 × 70.2 ft; Geared turbines,
Brown-Curtis-Fairfield; Twin
screw; 14,000 SHP; 16, max 17 kn;
Passengers: 542 cabin class, 1,268
3rd class; Crew: 390.

1920 Dec 14: Launched. Laid
down as *Montmorency*.
1922 Mar: Completed.
May 5: Maiden voyage Liverpool-
Montreal.
1928 Passenger accommodation:
cabin, tourist and 3rd class.
1929 May 29: First voyage
Hamburg-Montreal.
1931 New geared turbines fitted by
Harland & Wolff.
1932 Used almost exclusively for
cruising.
1939 Sep 12: Entered service as
armed merchant cruiser *Forfar*.
1940 Dec 2: HMS *Forfar* was
torpedoed and sunk by the German
submarine *U 99* west of Ireland in
position 55° 40′N-19° 00′W.

1 *Turbine steamer* Montcalm, *the first
of three sister ships for the
Liverpool-Canada service.*
2 *The* Montrose, *sunk in 1940 while
serving as an armed merchant cruiser.*

1

2

Turbine steamer *Montclare*
Canadian Pacific, Liverpool

Builders: Brown, Clydebank
Yard no: 465
16,314 GRT; 175.3 × 21.4 m /
575 × 70.2 ft; Geared turbines,
Brown-Curtis; Twin screw; 14,000
SHP; 16, max 17 kn; Passengers:
542 cabin class, 1,268 3rd class;
Crew: 390.

1921 Dec 18: Launched. Laid
down as *Metapedia*.
1922 Aug: Completed.
Aug 18: Maiden voyage Liverpool-
Montreal.
1928 Passenger accommodation:
cabin, tourist and 3rd class.
1929 New turbines fitted by
Harland & Wolff.
Mar 22: Antwerp-St John service.
Apr 17: Antwerp-Montreal service.
1930 Mar 20: First voyage
Hamburg-St John.
1933 Employed almost exclusively
for cruising until 1939.
1939 Aug 28: In service as armed
merchant cruiser.
1942 Apr: Conversion to
submarine depot-ship
commenced.
Jun 2: Sold to British Admiralty.
1955 Sep: Taken out of service.
1958 Feb 3: Arrived at
Inverkeithing. Broken up by T.W.
Ward.

Turbine steamer *Empress of
Canada*
Canadian Pacific, London

Builders: Fairfield, Glasgow
Yard no: 528
21,517 GRT; 198.0 × 23.6 m /
650 × 77.4 ft; Geared turbines,
Brown-Curtis-Fairfield; Twin
screw; 23,000 SHP; 18, max 20
kn; Passengers: 488 1st class, 106
2nd class, 238 3rd class, 926
Asiatic steerage; Crew: 530.

1920 Aug 17: Launched.
1922 May: Completed.
May 5: Maiden voyage Falmouth-
Hong Kong, then employed on
trans-Pacific service Vancouver-
Yokohama.
1928 Nov 1: From Vancouver to
Glasgow for fitting of new geared
turbines by Fairfield. 26,000 SHP,
21 kn, max 22.5 kn.
1929 Aug 28: One round voyage
Southampton-Quebec-
Southampton, then Vancouver-
Yokohama service again.
1939 Nov 29: Troop transport.
1943 While on a voyage from
Durban to England the *Empress of
Canada* was sunk by two torpedoes
from the Italian submarine
Leonardo da Vinci in the South
Atlantic in position 1° 13′ S-
9° 57′ W. 392 dead.

3 *The last ship of the trio, the*
Montclare.
4 *The* Empress of Canada, *which was
employed on the trans-Pacific service.*
5 *The* Empress of Canada *with white
hull after her refit in 1929.*

3

4

5

The New B-Class of P & O

Steamship *Ballarat*
P & O Line, Greenock

Builders: Harland & Wolff,
Greenock
Yard no: 348
13,065 GRT; 163.7 × 19.6 m /
537 × 64.3 ft; IV exp eng, Kincaid;
Twin screw; 9,500 IHP; 13.5, max
14.5 kn; Passengers: 490 3rd class,
700 steerage as necessary.

1920 Sep 14: Launched.
1921 Dec: Completed.
1922 Jan 27: Maiden voyage
London-Sydney.
1929 12,000 IHP after fitting of
auxiliary low pressure turbines. 15,
max 17 kn; 12,996 GRT.
Converted to oil-firing.
1935 Broken up at Briton Ferry.

Steamship *Baradine*
P & O Line, Belfast

Builders: Harland & Wolff, Belfast
Yard no: 583
13,144 GRT; 163.7 × 19.6 m /
537 × 64.3 ft; IV exp eng, H & W;
Twin screw; 9,500 IHP; 13.5, max
14.5 kn; Passengers; 490 3rd class,
695 steerage as necessary.

1920 Nov 27: Launched.
1921 Aug 18: Completed.
Sep 22: Maiden voyage London-
Sydney.
1929 12,000 IHP after fitting
of auxiliary low pressure turbines
and conversion to oil-firing. 15,
max 17 kn. 13,072 GRT.
1936 Broken up at Dalmuir.

1 *P & O liner* Ballarat. *The five ships of this class were a development of the pre-war B-Class.*
2 *Steamship* Baradine.

Steamship *Balranald*
P & O Line, Greenock

Builders: Harland & Wolff,
Greenock
Yard no: 349
13,039 GRT; 163.7 × 19.6 m /
537 × 64.3 ft; IV exp eng, Kincaid;
Twin screw; 9,500 IHP; 13.5, max
14.5 kn; Passengers: 490 3rd class,
700 steerage as necessary.

1921 Feb 24: Launched.
1922 Apr: Completed. London-
Sydney service.
1929 Fitted with auxiliary low
pressure turbines. Converted to
oil-firing. 12,000 IHP. 15, max 17
kn. 12,991 GRT.
May 10: First voyage after refit,
London-Sydney.
1936 Broken up at Troon.

Steamship *Barrabool*
P & O Line, Belfast

Builders: Harland & Wolff,
Belfast
Yard no: 584
13,148 GRT; 163.7 × 19.6 m /
537 × 64.3 ft; IV exp eng, H & W;
Twin screw; 9,500 IHP; 13.5, max
14.5 kn; Passengers: 490 3rd class,
700 steerage as necessary.

1921 Nov 3: Launched.
1922 Mar: Completed. London-
Sydney service.
1929 Fitted with auxiliary low
pressure turbines, and converted to
oil-firing 12,000 IHP. 15, max 17
kn. 13,062 GRT.
Sep 3: First voyage after refit,
London-Sydney.
1936 Sold to British Government
as troop transport. Sold again in
same year to be broken up at Bo'ness.

Steamship *Bendigo*
P & O Line, Greenock

Builders: Harland & Wolff,
Greenock
Yard no: 585
13,039 GRT; 163.7 × 19.6 m /
537 × 64.3 ft; IV exp eng, Kincaid;
Twin screw; 9,500 IHP; 13.5, max
14.5 kn; Passengers: 490 3rd class,
700 steerage as necessary.

1922 Jan 26: Launched.
Aug 9: Completed. London-
Sydney service.
1929 Auxiliary low pressure
turbines fitted and converted to oil-
firing. 12,000 IHP; 15, max 17 kn;
12,972 GRT.
1936 Broken up at Barrow.

3

3 *The* Balranald.

4

5

4 *The* Barrabool *sailed in P & O Branch Line's Australia service, as did her sister ships.*

5 Bendigo, *the last ship of the class, was broken up in 1936. Her four sister ships were also sold for breaking up during the years 1935/36.*

Turbine steamer *Alfonso XIII*
Cia Trasatlantica, Barcelona

1931 *Habana*
1964 *Galicia*

Builders: Soc Espanola de
Construction Naval, Bilbao
Yard no: 1
10,551 GRT; 152.4 × 18.6 m /
500 × 61.0 ft; Geared turbines,
from builders (Ferrol); Twin screw;
10,000 SHP; 16 kn; Passengers:
1,100 in three classes.

1920 Sep 14: Launched.
Oct 26: Badly damaged in a large
fire at the dockyard.
1923 Aug: Completed.
Sep 19: Maiden voyage Bilbao-
Vera Cruz.
1927 Jan: First voyage Bilbao-
Central America-New York.
1931 Renamed *Habana*.
1936 Jul: Laid up at Bordeaux
because of Spanish Civil War.
1939 Jun: Laid up at Bilbao.
Burnt out at Bilbao a few years
later. Repaired and refitted as
cargo vessel. 8,279 GRT.
1943 May 18: First voyage after
Civil War, Barcelona-New
Orleans.
1946/47 Refitted at Todd
Shipyards, New York.
Accommodation for 101 1st class
passengers. 10,069 GRT.
1947 Apr 16: First voyage New
York-Bilbao.
1953 8,279 GRT.
1960 Jul 26: Laid up at Ferrol.
1962 May 12: Sold to Pescanova
SA, Vigo. Converted at Ferrol to
fish-factory and refrigeration ship.
1964 Renamed *Galicia* after
conversion. 10,413 GRT.

Turbine steamer *Cristóbal Colón*
Cia Trasatlantica, Barcelona

Builders: Soc Espanola de
Construction Naval, Ferrol
Yard no: 5
10,833 GRT; 158.5 × 18.6 m /
520 × 61.0 ft; Geared turbines
from builders; Twin screw; 10,300
SHP; 16, max 16.5 kn; Passengers:
1,100 in three classes.

1921 Oct 31: Launched.
1923 Aug: Completed.
Bilbao-Central America service.
1927 Feb 2: First voyage Bilbao-
Central America-New York.
1936 Jul 25: The *Cristóbal Colón*
left New York bound for Bilbao.
On the way, the ship received
orders not to sail to Spain for the
time being because of the outbreak
of the Civil War but to
Southampton. From there the
liner went via Le Havre and St
Nazaire to Cardiff. In October the
Franco sympathisers among the
crew took over the ship, which had
left Cardiff for Vera Cruz on
October 18.
Oct 24: The *Cristóbal Colón*
stranded on North Rock off the
Bermudas and was declared a total
loss.

1 *The* Alfonso XIII, *the first ship of
over 10,000 GRT built in Spain.*
2 *The* Habana, *ex* Alfonso XIII, *after
the refit in 1943.*
3 *The* Cristóbal Colón *stranded off the
Bermudas in 1936.*

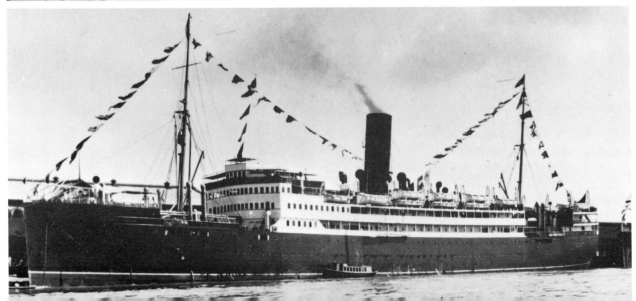

Six Purpose-built French Ships

Turbine steamer *Meduana*
Cie Sudatlantique, Bordeaux

1928 *Kerguelen*
1940 *Winrich von Kniprode*
1945 *Kerguelen*

Builders: Swan, Hunter & Wigham Richardson, Newcastle
Yard no: 1131
10,077 GRT; 152.1 × 18.0 m / 499 × 59.1 ft; Geared turbines, Wallsend Slipway; Twin screw; 6,500 SHP; 15 kn; Passengers: 100 1st class, 150 2nd class, 150 3rd class; 400 steerage; Crew: 170.

1920 Sep 30: Launched.
Nov 23: Burnt out and sank at fitting-out berth.
1921 Apr: Raised.
1922 Nov 23: Completed.
1923 Feb: Maiden voyage Bordeaux-South America.
1928 May: Sold to Chargeurs Réunis, Le Havre. Renamed *Kerguelen*. South America service. 10,123 GRT.
1940 Aug 6: Seized by German Navy. Renamed *Winrich von Kniprode*. Intended as Transport H 20 for Operation 'Sealion'.
1941 Managed as accommodation ship by F. Laeisz, Hamburg.
1945 Used in the Baltic for transporting the wounded.
Mar: Badly damaged in bombing attack at Pillau. Returned to Chargeurs Réunis at the end of 1945, and renamed *Kerguelen* once more.
1947 Repaired and refitted at Rotterdam and Bordeaux, the work lasting until 1948.
1948 Jun 10: First post-war voyage to South America. Later, Marseille-Indo-China service. 10,241 GRT.
1955 Feb: Sold to be broken up at Antwerp.

1 *Turbine steamer* Meduana *of the Cie Sudatlantique.*

1

2 *Chargeurs Réunis liner* Kerguelen *ex*
Meduana.
3 *The* Kerguelen *ex* Meduana *sailed
under the German flag during the
Second World War as the* Winrich von
Kniprode.

Turbine steamer *Mosella*
Cie Sudatlantique, Bordeaux

1928 *Jamaique*

Builders: Swan, Hunter & Wigham
Richardson, Newcastle
Yard no: 1145
10,250 GRT; 152.4 × 18.1 m /
500 × 59.4 ft; Geared turbines;
Wallsend Slipway; Twin screw;
6,500 SHP; 15 kn; Passengers: 100
1st class, 150 2nd class, 150 3rd
class, 400 steerage; Crew: 170.

1921 Sep 3: Launched.
1922 Apr: Completed. Bordeaux-
South America service.
1928 May: To Chargeurs Réunis,
Le Havre. Renamed *Jamaique*.
10,123 GRT.
Le Havre-La Plata ports service.
1947 Overhaul at St Nazaire.
1948 Jan 28: Le Havre-La Plata
service again.
1954 Nov: Sold to be broken up at
Ghent.

Turbine steamer *Chantilly*
Messageries Maritimes, Marseille

Launched as *Kerguelen*

Builders: Ch et A de la Loire, St
Nazaire
10,017 GRT; 152.6 × 18.1 m /
501 × 59.4 ft; Geared turbines,
Parsons-builders; Twin screw;
7,000 SHP; 15, max 16 kn;
Passengers: 130 1st class, 80 2nd
class; 116 3rd class, 254 steerage;
Crew: 175.

1922 Mar 14: Launched as
Kerguelen, intended for the South
America service of Chargeurs
Réunis, Le Havre.
1923 Jun: Bought by Messageries
Maritimes, Marseille. Renamed
Chantilly.
Dec: Completed.
1924 Jan 17: Maiden voyage
Marseille-Indo-China.
1925 9,986 GRT.
1940 May: Troop transport.
1941 Jan 1: Captured by British
warships near Tres Forcas. Served
as transport, from 1944 as hospital
ship. Managed by British India
Line. Home port Gibraltar.
1945 Handed back to Messageries
Maritimes.
Used in Indo-China service again.
1952 Oct: Sold to be broken up at
Marseille.

4 *The* Jamaique *ex* Mosella *in
Hamburg harbour in 1952.*
5 *The* Chantilly.

Turbine steamer *Aramis*
Messageries Maritimes, Marseille

1925 *Chenonceaux*

Builders: Ch et A de la Gironde, Bordeaux
Yard no: 178
14,644 GRT; 172.2 × 19.8 m / 565 × 65.0 ft; Geared turbines from builders; Twin screw; 9,000 SHP; 16 kn; Passengers: 101 1st class, 116 2nd class, 100 3rd class.

1922 Mar 30: Launched.
1923 Until 1924 there were various tests and improvements to the turbines, which were of a new design from the builders. As satisfactory operation was not achieved, the propulsion unit was taken out and replaced by the builders with triple expansion engines.
1925 Renamed *Chenonceaux*.
1926 Completed. 14,825 GRT, 14 kn.
1927 Mar: Marseille-Far East service.
1940 May: Troop transport to Norway, then laid up at Marseille.
1944 Aug: Sunk by German troops during the evacuation of Marseille.
1948 Apr: Raised.
Jun: To Toulon to be scrapped.

Turbine steamer *Compiégne*
Messageries Maritimes, Marseille

Launched as *Jamaique*

Builders: A et Ch de la Loire, St Nazaire
10,017 GRT; 152.6 × 18.1 m / 501 × 59.4 ft; Geared turbines, Parsons-builders; Twin screw; 7,000 SHP; 15, max 16 kn; Passengers: 130 1st class, 80 2nd class, 116 3rd class, 250 steerage; Crew: 175.

1922 Nov 18: Launched. Intended as the *Jamaique* for the South America service of Chargeurs Réunis, Le Havre.
1923 Jul: Bought by Messageries Maritimes. Renamed *Compiégne*.
1924 Feb: Completed.
Mar 13: Maiden voyage Marseille-Indo-China.
1925 9,986 GRT.
1941 Nov 3: Captured by British warships 200 nautical miles south of Durban. Entered service as transport under British flag.
1945 Nov 7: Handed back to Messageries Maritimes.
1946 Jul 22: Struck a mine 12 miles east of Dieppe. The sinking ship was beached.
Aug: Refloated and repaired at Dunkirk.
1948 May: Marseille-Far East service again.
1953 Sep 27: Laid up at Marseille.
1954 Apr 7: Sold to be broken up at La Seyne.

Turbine steamer *Fontainebleau*
Messageries Maritimes, Marseille

Builders: A et Ch de la Loire, St Nazaire
10,015 GRT; 152.6 × 18.1 m / 501 × 59.4 ft; Geared turbines, Parsons-builders; Twin screw; 7,000 SHP; 15, max 16 kn; Passengers: 130 1st class, 80 2nd class, 116 3rd class, 250 steerage; Crew: 170.

1923 Nov 9: Launched. The ship was laid down as the *Islande* for the South America service of Chargeurs Réunis, Le Havre. Sold to Messageries Maritimes in 1923.
1924 Aug: Completed.
Sep 18: Maiden voyage Marseille-Far East.
1926 Jul 12: While on a voyage Marseille-Yokohama the *Fontainebleau* was completely burnt out at Djibouti. The wreck was sunk to form the foundation for a breakwater.

6 *The steamship* Chenonceaux, *originally built as turbine steamer* Aramis.
7 *The* Compiégne, *of Messageries Maritimes.*
8 *The* Fontainebleau.

6

7

8

Turbine steamer *Calchas*
Blue Funnel Line, Liverpool

Builders: Workman, Clark & Co, Belfast
Yard no: 357
10,304 GRT; 156.5 × 19.0 m / 513 × 62.3 ft; Geared turbines, Brown-Curtis-builders; Twin screw; 6,500 SHP; 14.5 kn; Passengers: numbers not available.

1921 Jan 11: launched.
Jun 4: Completed. Liverpool-Far East service.
1941 Apr 21: The *Calchas* was torpedoed and sunk by the German submarine *U 107* in the Atlantic off West Africa in position 23° 50′N-27° 00′W. 31 dead.

Turbine steamer *Diomed*
Blue Funnel Line, Liverpool

Builders: Workman, Clark & Co, Belfast
Yard no: 392
10,354 GRT; 156.5 × 19.0 m / 513 × 62.3 ft; Geared turbines, Brown-Curtis-builders; Twin screw; 6,500 SHP; 14.5 kn; Passengers: numbers not available.

1922 Jan 14: Launched.
May 16: Completed. Liverpool-Far East service.
1952 Sep: Sold to be broken up at Dalmuir.

Turbine steamer *Perseus*
Blue Funnel Line, Liverpool

Builders: Caledon SB & E Co, Dundee
Yard no: 259
10,276 GRT; 156.5 × 19.0 m / 513 × 62.3 ft; Geared turbines, Parsons; Twin screw; 6,500 SHP; 14.5 kn; Passengers: numbers not available.

1922 Aug 23: Launched.
1923 Feb: Completed. Liverpool-Far East service.
1944 Jan 16: The *Perseus* was torpedoed and sunk by the Japanese submarine *I 165* in the Gulf of Bengal near Madras in position 12° 00′N-80° 14′E.

Turbine steamer *Menelaus*
Blue Funnel Line, Liverpool

Builders: Caledon SB & E Co, Dundee
Yard no: 274
10,278 GRT; 157.4 × 19.0 m / 516 × 62.3 ft; Geared turbines, NE Marine Eng Co; Twin screw; 6,500 SHP; 14.5 kn; Passengers: numbers not available.

1923 May 1: launched.
Oct 11: Completed. Liverpool-Far East service.
1952 Jun: Sold to be broken up at Dalmuir.

1

1-4 *The four turbine steamers built for the Liverpool-Far East service,* Calchas *(1),* Diomed *(2),* Perseus *in picture 3 as an armed merchantman in 1943, and* Menelaus *(4).*

2

3

4

Turbine steamer *Sarpedon*
Blue Funnel Line, Liverpool

Builders: Cammell Laird & Co,
Birkenhead
Yard no: 893
11,321 GRT; 161.6 × 19.0 m /
530 × 62.3 ft; Geared turbines,
Brown-Curtis-builders; Twin
screw; 8,000 SHP; 15, max 15.5
kn; Passengers: 155 1st class;
Crew: 80.

1923 Feb 2: Launched.
May 15: Completed.
Jun 9: Maiden voyage
Liverpool-Far East.
1946 Jan 5: First voyage
Liverpool-Brisbane.
1953 Jun: Sold to J. Cashmore,
Newport, Mon, to be broken up.

Turbine steamer *Patroclus*
Blue Funnel Line, Liverpool

Builders: Scott's, Greenock
Yard no: 518
11,314 GRT; 161.5 × 19.0 m /
530 × 62.3 ft; Geared turbines,
Scott's; Twin screw; 8,000 SHP;
15, max 15.5 kn; Passengers: 140
1st class; Crew: 80.

1923 Mar 17: Launched.
Jun: Completed.
Liverpool-Far East service.
1939 Entered service as armed
merchant cruiser.
1940 Nov 4: The *Patroclus* was
torpedoed by the German
submarine *U 99* 150 nautical miles
west of Ireland while rescuing
survivors from the British armed
merchant cruiser *Laurentic*, which
had been torpedoed a few hours
earlier. The *Patroclus* did not go
down until five hours later after five
further torpedo hits, because her
holds were filled with empty
barrels, making her almost
unsinkable. This was in position
53° 43′N-14° 41′W. 76 dead.

Turbine steamer *Hector*
Blue Funnel Line, Liverpool

Builders: Scott's, Greenock
Yard no: 521
11,198 GRT; 161.5 × 19.0 m /
530 × 62.3 ft; Geared turbines,
Scott's; Twin screw; 8,000 SHP;
15, max 15.5 kn; Passengers: 175
1st class; Crew 80.

1924 Jun 18: Launched.
Sep 24: Completed.
Liverpool-Far East service.
1940 Entered service as armed
merchant cruiser.
1942 Apr 5: The *Hector* was sunk
in the harbour of Colombo during a
Japanese air raid.
1946 The wreck was raised and
scrapped.

Turbine steamer *Antenor*
Blue Funnel Line, Liverpool

Builders: Palmers, Newcastle
Yard no: 945
11,174 GRT; 161.6 × 19.0 m /
530 × 62.3 ft; Geared turbines,
Parsons Palmers; Twin screw;
8,000 SHP; 15, max 15.5 kn;
Passengers: 182 1st class; Crew 80.
1924 Sep 30: Launched.
1925 Jan 15: Completed.
Liverpool-Far East service.
1953 Jul: Sold to British Iron &
Steel Corp and broken up at Blyth.

5

5 *The turbine steamers* Sarpedon (5),
Patroclus (6), Hector (7) *and* Antenor
(8) *formed a second series of four, also
for the Blue Funnel Line's Far East
service.*

6

7

8

Vandyck and Voltaire

Turbine steamer *Vandyck*
Lamport & Holt, Liverpool

Builders: Workman, Clark & Co,
Belfast
Yard no: 359
13,233 GRT; 170.3 × 19.6 m /
559 × 64.3 ft; Geared turbines
from builders; Twin screw; 7,000
SHP; 14.5 kn; Passengers: 300 1st
class, 150 2nd class, 230 3rd class.

1921 Feb 24: Launched.
Sep 27: Completed. New York-La
Plata ports service.
1930 Laid up at Southampton.
1932 In service again as cruise
liner. White hull.
1939 Oct: Troop transport.
1940 Jun 11: The *Vandyck* was
sunk by German aircraft north of
Harstad, Norway. Various British
publications give June 10 as the
date of the sinking. According to
Laurence Dunn the *Vandyck* was
sunk on June 9. The date June 11 is
taken from 'Chronik des
Seekrieges 1939-1945', by
Rohwer/Hümmelchen.

Steamship *Voltaire*
Lamport & Holt, Liverpool

Builders: Workman Clark & Co,
Belfast
Yard no: 360
13,248 GRT; 170.3 × 19.6 m /
559 × 64.3 ft; IV exp eng from
builders; Twin screw; 7,500 IHP;
14.5, max 15 kn; Passengers: 300
1st class, 150 2nd class, 230 3rd
class.

1923 Aug 14: Launched.
Nov 22: Completed. Entered New
York-La Plata ports service.
1930 Laid up on River Blackwater.
1932 Entered service as cruise
liner. White hull.
1939 Armed merchant cruiser.
1941 Apr 4: The *Voltaire* engaged
the German auxiliary cruiser *Thor*
in mid-Atlantic. After an exchange
of fire lasting one hour, the
Voltaire, already burning fiercely,
was unmanoeuvrable and could not
fight any longer. Half an hour later
she sank in position 14° 25′N-
40° 40′W. 75 British seamen had
died. 197 survivors were taken on
board the *Thor*.

1

2

1 *Lamport & Holt liner* Vandyck.
2 *The* Voltaire *as cruise liner in the
'30s.*

Cunard A-Liners

Turbine steamer *Antonia*
Cunard Line, Liverpool

1944 *Wayland*

Builders: Vickers, Barrow
Yard no: 498
13,867 GRT; 164.6 × 19.9 m /
540 × 65.2 ft; Geared turbines,
Vickers; Twin screw; 8,500 SHP;
15 kn; Passengers: 484 cabin class,
1,222 3rd class; Crew: 271.

1921 Mar 11: Launched.
1922 Jun 3: Completed.
Jun 15: Maiden voyage
Southampton-Montreal.
1928 First voyage
Liverpool-Montreal.
1940 Oct: Entered service as
armed merchant cruiser.
1942 Mar 24: Sold to British
Admiralty. Converted to repair-
ship.
1944 Placed in service as HMS
Wayland.
1948 Broken up in Scotland.

Turbine steamer *Ausonia*
Cunard Line, Liverpool

Builders: Armstrong Whitworth,
Newcastle.
Yard no: 970
13,912 GRT; 164.0 × 19.9 m /
538 × 65.3 ft; Geared turbines
from builders; Twin screw; 8,500
SHP; 15 kn; Passengers: 510 cabin
class, 1,178 3rd class; Crew: 270.

1921 Mar 22: Launched.
Jun: Completed.
Aug 31: Maiden voyage
Liverpool-Montreal.
1923 First voyage
London-Montreal.
1939 Sep 2: Fitted out as armed
merchant cruiser.
1942 Jun 3: Sold to British
Admiralty. Converted to repair-
ship.
1945 Laid up.
1958 To Malta as repair-ship for
the Mediterranean fleet.
1964 Sep: Laid up at Portsmouth.
1965 Aug: Sold to be broken up at
Castellon.

1 *Cunard Line built six new ships
between 1921 and 1926 to replace the
A-Class ships lost during the First
World War. The* Antonia *made her
maiden voyage to Canada in 1922.*
2 *Cunard liner* Ausonia.

1

2

Turbine steamer *Andania*
Cunard Line, Liverpool

Builders: Hawthorn, Leslie & Co,
Newcastle
Yard no: 500
13,950 GRT; 164.0 × 19.9 m /
538 × 65.3 ft; Geared turbines
from builders; Twin screw: 8,500
SHP; 15 kn; Passengers: 484 cabin
class, 1,222 3rd class; Crew: 270.

1921 Nov 1: Launched.
1922 May 24: Completed.
Jun 1: Maiden voyage
Southampton-Montreal.
1925 First voyage Hamburg-New
York.
1927 Liverpool-Montreal service.
1939 Sep: Fitted out as armed
merchant cruiser.
1940 Jun 16: The *Andania* was
torpedoed and sunk by the German
submarine *U A* 70 nautical miles
from Reykjavik in position
62° 36′N-15° 00′W. (The date of
sinking given in British sources,
June 15, is correct according to
British time. In German time the
attack occurred on the 16th at
00.27 hours.)

Turbine steamer *Ascania*
Cunard Line, Liverpool

Builders: Armstrong Whitworth,
Newcastle
Yard no: 971
14,013 GRT; 164.1 × 19.9 m /
538 × 65.3 ft; Geared turbines
from builders; Twin screw; 8,500
SHP; 15 kn; Passengers: 500 cabin
class, 1,200 3rd class; Crew: 270.

1923 Dec 20: Launched.
1924 Building halted for several
months because of excessive wage
and material costs.
1925 May 2: Completed.
May 22: Maiden voyage
London-Montreal.
1939 Aug 24: Fitted out as armed
merchant cruiser.
1943 Apr 21: Placed in service as
troop transport.
1947 Dec 20: First post-war voyage
Liverpool-Halifax.
1949/50 Overhaul and refit.
14,440 GRT. Passengers: 198 1st
class, 498 tourist class.
1950 Apr 21: Liverpool-Montreal
service.

1957 Jan 1: Arrived at Newport,
Mon. Broken up by J. Cashmore.

3

3 *The launching of the* Andania.
4 *The* Andania *was sunk in 1940 while
serving as an auxiliary cruiser.*
5 *Turbine steamer* Ascania *in the Irish
Sea in 1948.*

4

5

Turbine steamer *Aurania*
Cunard Line, Liverpool

1944 *Artifex*

Builders: Swan, Hunter & Wigham
Richardson, Newcastle
Yard no: 1127
13,984 GRT; 164.6 × 19.9 m /
540 × 65.2 ft; Geared turbines,
Wallsend Slipway; Twin screw;
8,500 SHP; 15 kn; Passengers: 500
cabin class, 1,200 3rd class; Crew:
270.

1924 Feb 6: Launched.
Sep 6: Completed.
Sep 13: Maiden voyage
Liverpool-New York.
1925 Liverpool-Montreal service.
1928 London-Montreal service.
1939 Aug 24: Fitted out as armed
merchant cruiser.
1942 Mar 9: Sold to British
Admiralty. Converted to repair ship.
1944 Entered service as HMS
Artifex.
1961 Jan: Sold to be broken up at
La Spezia.

Turbine steamer *Alaunia*
Cunard Line, Liverpool

Builders: Brown, Clydebank
Yard no: 495
14,030 GRT; 164.0 × 19.9 m /
538 × 65.3 ft; Geared turbines
from builders; Twin screw; 8,500
SHP; 15 kn; Passengers: 484 cabin
class, 1,222 3rd class; Crew: 270.

1925 Feb 7: Launched.
Jul: Completed.
Jul 24: Maiden voyage
Liverpool-Montreal.
1926 London-Montreal service.
1939 Aug 24: Fitted out as armed
merchant cruiser.
1941 Troop transport.
1944 Dec 8: Sold to British
Admiralty. Conversion to
repair-ship commenced, which
took until August 1945.
1957 Sep: To Hughes, Bolckow,
Blyth, to be broken up.

6/7 The Aurania *as Cunard liner (6) and as armed merchant cruiser (7).*
8 The last ship of the class to enter service, the Alaunia.

6

Turbine steamer *Moreton Bay*
Commonwealth Government Line,
Brisbane

Builders: Vickers, Barrow
Yard no: 573
13,850 GRT; 167.2 × 20.8 m /
549 × 68.2 ft; Geared turbines,
Vickers; Twin screw; 9,000 SHP;
15 kn; Passengers: 12 1st class, 712
3rd class; Crew: 216.

1921 Apr 23: Launched.
Nov 18: Completed.
Dec 7: Maiden voyage
London-Brisbane.
1928 Sold to the White Star Line.
Registered at London and
managed by the Aberdeen Line.
Continued in same service.
1931 14,145 GRT. Passengers:
542 tourist class.
1933 A group of British shipping
companies founded the Aberdeen
& Commonwealth Line, which
took over the *Moreton Bay* and her
sister ships from White Star Line
which was in difficulties.
1939 Aug: Fitted out as armed
merchant cruiser.

1941 Aug: Troop transport. After
the war, in Australia service again,
London-Sydney.
1948 14,376 GRT.
1957 Apr 13: Arrived at Barrow.
Broken up by T.W. Ward.

Turbine steamer *Largs Bay*
Commonwealth Government Line,
Adelaide

Builders: Beardmore, Glasgow
Yard no: 616
13,851 GRT; 168.3 × 20.8 m /
552 × 68.2 ft; Geared turbines,
Parsons-builders; Twin screw;
9,000 SHP; 15 kn; Passengers: 12
1st class, 710 3rd class; Crew: 215.

1921 Jun 20: Launched.
Dec: Completed.
1922 Jan 4: Maiden voyage
London-Brisbane.
1928 Sold to the White Star Line.
Registered at London and
managed by the Aberdeen Line.
Continued in Australia service.
1931 14,184 GRT. Passengers:
550 tourist class.
1933 To Aberdeen &
Commonwealth Line, London.
1941 Aug: Troop transport.
1948/49 Overhaul and refit.
14,362 GRT. 290 tourist class
passengers.
1949 London-Sydney service.
1957 Apr: Sold to be broken up at
Barrow.

1

1 *Commonwealth Government liner*
Moreton Bay *in 1921.*
2 *The* Moreton Bay *in the '50s.*
3 *The* Largs Bay *after her 1949 refit.*

Turbine steamer *Hobsons Bay*
Commonwealth Government Line,
Melbourne

1936 *Esperance Bay*

Builders: Vickers, Barrow
Yard no: 574
13,837 GRT; 167.2 × 20.8 m /
549 × 68.2 ft; Geared turbines,
Vickers; Twin screw; 9,000 SHP;
15 kn; Passengers: 12 1st class, 738
3rd class; Crew: 215.

1921 Oct 4: Launched.
1922 Jan: Completed.
Feb 28: Maiden voyage
London-Brisbane.
1928 Sold to the White Star Line.
Registered at London and
managed by the Aberdeen Line.
Continued in Australia service.
1931 14,198 GRT. Passengers:
512 tourist class.
1933 To Aberdeen &
Commonwealth Line, London.
1936 Renamed *Esperance Bay*.
1939 Sep: Fitted out at Brisbane as
armed merchant cruiser.
1941 Troop transport. Australia
service London-Sydney again after
the war.
1948 14,343 GRT. Passengers:
290 tourist class.
1955 Jul 6: Arrived at Faslane.
Broken up by Shipbreaking
Industries.

Turbine steamer *Esperance Bay*
Commonwealth Government Line,
Freemantle

1936 *Arawa*

Builders: Beardmore, Glasgow
Yard no: 617
13,853 GRT; 168.3 × 20.8 m /
552 × 68.2 ft; Geared turbines,
Parsons-builders; Twin screw;
9,000 SHP; 15 kn; Passengers: 12
1st class, 720 3rd class; Crew: 216.

1921 Dec 15: Launched.
1922 Jul 11: Completed.
Aug 1: Maiden voyage London-
Brisbane.
1928 Sold to the White Star
Line. Registered at London and
managed by the Aberdeen Line.
1931 14,176 GRT. Passengers:
550 tourist class.
1933 To Aberdeen &
Commonwealth Line, London.
1936 Sold to Shaw, Savill &
Albion, Southampton.
14,462 GRT after refit.
Passengers: 292 tourist class.
1937 Jan 22: First voyage
Southampton-Wellington.
1939 Oct 17: Entered service as
armed merchant cruiser.
1941 Troop transport.
1946 Feb 7: First post-war voyage
London-New Zealand. 14,491
GRT. 274 tourist class passengers.
1955 May: Sold to J. Cashmore,
Newport, Mon, to be broken up.

Turbine steamer *Jervis Bay*
Commonwealth Government Line,
Sydney

Builders: Vickers, Barrow
Yard no: 575
13,839 GRT; 167.2 × 20.8 m /
549 × 68.2 ft; Geared turbines,
Vickers; Twin screw; 9,000 SHP;
15 kn; Passengers: 12 1st class, 700
3rd class; Crew: 216.

1922 Jan 17: Launched.
Sep: Completed.
Sep 26: Maiden voyage
London-Brisbane.
1928 Sold to the White Star Line.
Registered at London and
managed by the Aberdeen Line.
1931 14,164 GRT. Passengers:
542 tourist class.
1933 To Aberdeen &
Commonwealth Line, London.
1939 Sep: Fitted out as armed
merchant cruiser.
1940 Nov 5: The British convoy
HX 84, consisting of 37 ships
escorted solely by the armed
merchant cruiser *Jervis Bay*, was
attacked in the North Atlantic by
the German heavy cruiser *Admiral
Scheer*. The hopelessly out-gunned
Jervis Bay fought bravely until the
end, allowing the main body of the
convoy to escape. Six ships were
sunk in addition to the *Jervis Bay*.

4 *The* Esperance Bay *ex* Hobsons Bay.
5 *Shaw Savill & Albion liner* Arawa,
the former Esperance Bay.
6 *The* Jervis Bay *during trials. The*
Jervis Bay *was sunk in 1940 after a
courageous fight with the German
heavy cruiser* Admiral Scheer.

4

5

6

The H-Class of Nippon Yusen KK

Turbine steamer *Hakone Maru*
Nippon Yusen KK, Tokyo

Builders: Mitsubishi, Nagasaki
Yard no: 346
10,423 GRT; 158.5 × 18.9 m /
520 × 62.0 ft; Geared turbines,
Parsons-builders; Twin screw;
9,600 SHP; 15, max 16 kn;
Passengers: 175 1st class; Crew:
200.

1921 Jul 25: Launched.
Oct 31: Delivered. Yokohama-
Hamburg service.
1943 Nov 27: The *Hakone Maru*
was sunk by US aircraft in the
straits of Formosa.

Turbine steamer *Haruna Maru*
Nippon Yusen KK, Tokyo

Builders: Mitsubishi, Nagasaki
Yard no: 347
10,421 GRT; 158.5 × 18.9 m /
520 × 62.0 ft; Geared turbines,
Parsons-builders; Twin screw;
9,600 SHP; 15, max 16 kn;
Passengers: 175 1st class; Crew:
200.

1921 Nov 5: Launched.
1922 Jan 31: Delivered.
Yokohama-Hamburg service.
1942 Jul 7: Stranded off Surga
Bay. Total loss.

1 *The* Hakone Maru *at Hamburg in
1936.*
2 *The* Haruna Maru.

1

2

Turbine steamer *Hakozaki Maru*
Nippon Yusen KK, Tokyo

Builders: Mitsubishi, Nagasaki
Yard no: 348
10,413 GRT; 158.5 × 18.9 m /
520 × 62.0 ft; Geared turbines,
Parsons-builders; Twin screw;
9,600 SHP; 15, max 16 kn;
Passengers: 175 1st class; Crew:
200.

1922 Mar 2: Launched.
Jun 1: Delivered. Yokohama-
Hamburg service.
1940 Troop transport with
Japanese navy.
1945 Mar 19: The *Hakozaki Maru*
was torpedoed and sunk by the
American submarine *Balao* in the
East China Sea in position
32° 10′N-122° 10′E.

Turbine steamer *Hakusan Maru*
Nippon Yusen KK, Tokyo

Builders: Mitsubishi, Nagasaki
Yard no: 383
10,380 GRT; 158.5 × 18.9 m /
520 × 62.0 ft: Geared turbines,
Parsons-builders; Twin screw;
9,600 SHP; 15, max 16 kn;
Passengers: 175 1st class; Crew:
200.

1923 May 19: Launched.
Sep 20: Delivered. Yokohama-
Hamburg service.
1940 Troop transport with
Japanese navy.
1944 Jun 4: The *Hakusan Maru*
was torpedoed and sunk by the US
submarine *Flier* southwest of
Iwojima in position 22° 55′N-
136° 44′E.

3

4

3 *The* Hakozaki Maru *in her early
years of service with the old black NYK
funnel.*
4 *Turbine steamer* Hakusan Maru.

Turbine steamer *City of Paris*
Ellerman Lines, Glasgow

Builders: Swan, Hunter & Wigham
Richardson, Newcastle
Yard no: 1129
10,902 GRT; 153.6 × 18.1 m /
504 × 59.4 ft; Geared turbines,
Wallsend Slipway; Single screw;
6,500 SHP; 15 kn; Passengers: 230
1st class, 100 2nd class; Crew: 190.

1921 Launched. Because of a
strike at the shipyard the ship was
subsequently sent to St Nazaire for
final fitting-out by Penhoët.
1922 Feb: Completed. Maiden
voyage London-Far East, followed
by service from British ports to
India.
1936 London-Cape Town-Beira
service.
1938 Passengers: 199 in two
classes.
1941 Sep: Troop transport.
1944/45 Accommodation ship,

then troop transport again.
1947 Returned to Ellerman Lines.
Overhauled and refitted at
Newcastle.
New funnel. 10,877 GRT. London-
Africa service.
1956 Feb 24: Arrived at Newport,
Mon, to be broken up by J.
Cashmore.

Steamship *City of Nagpur*
Ellerman Lines, Glasgow

Builders: Workman, Clark & Co,
Belfast
Yard no: 464
10,138 GRT; 149.5 × 18.0 m /
490 × 59.1 ft; IV exp eng from
builders; Single screw; 6,000 IHP;
15 kn; Passengers: 226 1st class, 92
2nd class; Crew: 190.

1922 May 30: Launched.
Sep 12: Completed.
Oct 12: Maiden voyage Glasgow-
Bombay.
1933 Laid up at Bombay.
1934 London-Africa service.
1936 Used for cruises during
summer months until 1939.
1938 Modernisation of passenger
accommodation by Gray & Co,
West Hartlepool. 10,146 GRT.
1941 Apr 29: The *City of Nagpur*
was torpedoed and sunk by the
German submarine *U 75* 700
nautical miles west of Fastnet. 14
dead.

1

2

3

1 *The* City of Paris, *original external appearance.*
2 *The* City of Paris *after her 1947 refit.*
3 *Ellerman liner* City of Nagpur.

Sophocles and Diogenes

Turbine steamer *Sophocles*
Aberdeen Line, Aberdeen

1926 *Tamaroa*

Builders: Harland & Wolff, Belfast
Yard no: 575
12,361 GRT; 158.1 × 19.3 m /
519 × 63.3 ft; Geared turbines,
Brown-Curtis-H & W; Twin screw;
5,200 SHP; 13.5 kn; Passengers:
131 1st class, 422 3rd class.

1921 Sep 22: Launched.
1922 Feb 2: Completed.
Mar 1: Maiden voyage
London-Brisbane.
1926 Chartered to Shaw, Savill &
Albion. Renamed *Tamaroa*.
Converted to oil-firing. 15 kn.
12,354 GRT.
Sep 10: First voyage Southampton-
Wellington.
1931 Passengers: 130 cabin class.
1932 Bought by Shaw, Savill &
Albion, Southampton. 12,405
GRT.
1940 Nov: Troop transport.
1948 Aug 27: London-Wellington
service. 12,375 GRT. Passengers:
372 tourist class.
1957 Mar 5: Arrived at Blyth to be
broken up by Hughes, Bolckow.

Turbine steamer *Diogenes*
Aberdeen Line, Aberdeen

1926 *Mataroa*

Builders: Harland & Wolff, Belfast
Yard no: 576
12,341 GRT; 158.1 × 19.3 m /
519 × 63.3 ft; Geared turbines,
Brown-Curtis-H & W; Twin screw;
5,200 SHP; 13.5 kn; Passengers:
131 1st class, 422 3rd class.

1922 Mar 2: Launched.
May 16: Completed.
Jul 4: Delivered.
Aug 16: Maiden voyage
London-Brisbane.
1926 Chartered to Shaw, Savill &
Albion. Renamed *Mataroa*.
Converted to oil-firing. 15 kn.
12,333 GRT.
Nov 5: First voyage Southampton-
Wellington.
1931 Passengers: 131 cabin class.
1932 Bought by Shaw, Savill &
Albion, Southampton. 12,390
GRT.
1940 Nov: Troop transport.
1948 Apr 30: London-Wellington
service. 12,369 GRT. Passengers:
372 tourist class.

1957 Mar 29: Arrived at Faslane.
Broken up by BISCO.

1 *Turbine steamer* Tamaroa *ex*
Sophocles.
2 *Aberdeen liner* Diogenes.
3 *The* Mataroa *ex* Diogenes.

1

Turbine steamer *Moldavia*
P & O Line, Liverpool

Builders: Cammell Laird & Co,
Birkenhead
Yard no: 839
16,277 GRT; 174.6 × 21.8 m /
573 × 71.5 ft; Geared turbines
from builders; Twin screw; 13,250
SHP; 16 kn; Passengers: 222 1st
class, 175 2nd class; Crew: 350.

1921 Oct 1: Launched.
1922 Sep 19: Completed.
Oct 13: Maiden voyage
London-Bombay.
1923 Feb 16: First voyage London-
Sydney.
1925 16,436 GRT.
1928 Refit. Second funnel fitted.
Passenger accommodation; 2nd
class now 3rd class. 16,543 GRT.
1931 Passenger accommodation
for 830 tourist class. 16,556 GRT.
1938 Broken up.

1/2 *The* Moldavia *was the first P & O
Line turbine steamer. In 1928 the ship
received a second, dummy funnel.*

Turbine steamer *Mongolia*
P & O Line, Newcastle

1938 *Rimutaka*
1950 *Europa*
1951 *Nassau*
1961 *Acapulco*

Builders: Armstrong Whitworth,
Newcastle
Yard no: 964
16,385 GRT; 173.2 × 21.9 m /
568 × 71.9 ft; Geared turbines
from builders; Twin screw; 13,000
SHP; 16 kn; Passengers: 230 1st
class, 180 2nd class; Crew: 353.

1922 Aug 24: Launched.
1923 Apr 25: Completed.
May 11: Maiden voyage
London-Sydney.
1928 2nd class passenger
accommodation now 3rd class.
16,504 GRT.
1931 Passengers: 800 tourist class.
16,596 GRT.

1938 Chartered to New Zealand
Line. Home port Plymouth.
Dec 8: First voyage
London-Wellington.
1950 Feb: Sold to Cia de Nav
Incres SA, Panama. Renamed
Europa. 500 tourist class
passengers. 15,044 GRT.
Jul 5: First voyage New
York-Antwerp.
1951 Renamed *Nassau*. New York-
Nassau service.
1954 Transferred to Incres SS Co,
Monrovia.
1961 Sold to Cia Nav Turistica
Mexicana SA, Acapulco. Renamed
Acapulco.
Refitted and modernised by
Fairfield, Glasgow. 15,182 GRT.
Overall length 177.0 m / 575 ft.
Employed on cruising.
1963 May 19: Laid up at
Manzanilla.
1964 Dec 15: Arrived at Osaka to
be broken up.

3

4

5

3 *P & O Liner* Mongolia *in Hamburg
harbour.*
4 *The* Nassau *of the Incres SS Co.*
5 *In 1961 the former* Mongolia *was
sold to Mexico and entered service as
the* Acapulco *after an extensive refit.*

Steamship *Mooltan*
P & O Line, Belfast

Builders: Harland & Wolff,
Belfast
Yard no: 587
20,847 GRT; 190.5 × 22.3 m /
625 × 73.2 ft; IV exp eng, H & W;
Twin screw; 16,000 IHP; 16 kn;
Passengers: 327 1st class, 329 2nd
class.

1923 Feb 15: Launched.
Sep 21: Completed.
Dec 21: Maiden voyage London-
Sydney.
1929 Engine performance
improved by fitting of auxiliary low
pressure turbo-electric machinery.
17, max 17.5 kn. 20,952 GRT.
1939 Oct: Entered service as
armed merchant cruiser. Main
mast removed.
1941 Troop transport.
1947 Overhauled and refitted by
Harland & Wolff.
1948 Aug 26: First post-war
voyage London-Sydney. 21,039
GRT. 1,030 tourist class
passengers.

1954 Jan: To Faslane to be broken
up.

Steamship *Maloja*
P & O Line, Belfast

Builders: Harland & Wolff, Belfast
Yard no: 588
20,837 GRT; 190.5 × 22.3 m /
625 × 73.2 ft; IV exp eng, H & W;
Twin screw; 16,000 IHP; 16 kn;
Passengers: 327 1st class, 329 2nd
class.

1923 Apr 19: Launched.
Oct 25: Completed.
Nov: Maiden voyage
London-Bombay.
1924 Jan 18: First voyage
London-Sydney.
1929 Auxiliary low pressure
turbines fitted. 17, max 17.5 kn;
20, 914 GRT.
1939 Oct: Entered service as
armed merchant cruiser.
1941 Troop transport.
1947 Overhauled and refitted at
London.

1948 Jun 10: First post-war voyage
London-Sydney. 21,036 GRT.
1,030 tourist class passengers.
1954 Apr: To Inverkeithing to be
broken up.

6

6 *P & O Line's* Mooltan *about 1930.*
7 *Steamship* Mooltan *after her 1947
refit.*
8 *The* Maloja *in her last years of
service.*

7

8

Antonio Delfino and Cap Norte

Steamship *Antonio Delfino*
Hamburg-South America Line,
Hamburg

1932 *Sierra Nevada*
1934 *Antonio Delfino*
1946 *Empire Halladale*

Builders: 'Vulcan', Hamburg
Yard no: 631
13,589 GRT; 160.4 × 19.5 m /
526 × 64.0 ft; III exp eng, Vulcan;
Twin screw; 6,300 IHP; 13.5 kn;
Passengers: 184 1st class, 334 2nd
class, 1,368 steerage; Crew: 211.

1921 Nov 10: Launched.
1922 Mar: Completed.
Mar 16: Maiden voyage
Hamburg-La Plata ports.
1927 Low pressure turbines fitted.
8,300 IHP, 15 kn.
1932 Chartered to North German
Lloyd. Renamed *Sierra Nevada*.
1934 *Antonio Delfino* again,
Hamburg-South America Line.

1939 Sep: Slipped out of Bahia.
Broke through the blockade to
Germany.
1940 Apr 17: Accommodation
ship for the German navy at Kiel.
1943 Moved to Gotenhafen
(Gdynia).
1945 Took part in the evacuation
of the German eastern territories.
In five operations she transported
20,500 people to the west.
May: Seized by Great Britain at
Copenhagen. Refitted as troop
transport. 14,056 GRT.
Passengers: 200 cabin class. 843
troops.
1946 Oct 4: Entered service as
Empire Halladale, managed by
Anchor Line, London, for the
Ministry of Transport.
1955 Oct 30: Laid up.
1956 Feb 1: To Arnott Young,
Dalmuir, to be broken up.

1

1/2 The Antonio Delfino *came into
service in 1922. She was the first large
new ship of Hamburg-South America
Line after the war.*
3 MOT troopship Empire Halladale *ex*
Antonio Delfino.

2

3

Steamship *Cap Norte*
Hamburg-South America Line,
Hamburg

1932 *Sierra Salvada*
1934 *Cap Norte*
1940 *Empire Trooper*

Builders: 'Vulcan', Hamburg
Yard no: 632
13,615 GRT; 160.4 × 19.5 m /
526 × 64.0 ft; III exp eng, Vulcan;
Twin screw; 6,300 IHP; 13.5 kn;
Passengers: 184 1st class, 334 3rd
class, 1,368 steerage; Crew: 211.

1922 May 8: Launched.
Aug 22: Completed.
Sep 14: Maiden voyage Hamburg-
La Plata ports.
1927 Low pressure turbines fitted.
8,300 IHP, 15 kn.
1932 Chartered to North German
Lloyd. Renamed *Sierra Salvada*.
1934 *Cap Norte* again,
Hamburg-South America Line.

1939 Oct 9: While trying to break
out of Pernambuco to Hamburg.
the ship was intercepted off Iceland
by the British cruiser *Belfast*. Due
to the bad weather the captain did
not give the order to scuttle the
ship. *Cap Norte* became a British
war prize.
1940 Jun: Refitted as troop
transport at Newcastle. Managed
by British India Line for Ministry
of War Transport. Renamed
Empire Trooper.
Dec 25: Badly damaged by gunfire
from the cruiser *Admiral Hipper*
while sailing in convoy. Made for
Punta Delgada as a port of refuge.
1949 Refitted at Falmouth. 14,106
GRT. Accommodation for 336
cabin passengers and 924 troops.
1955 Apr: Sold to British Iron and
Steel Corp to be broken up.
May: Caught fire and sank at
Inverkeithing.
Jun 19: Wreck raised. Scrapped.

4 *Hamburg-South America steamer*
Cap Norte. *Photo taken about 1935.*

Athenia and Letitia

Turbine steamer *Athenia*
Anchor-Donaldson Line, Glasgow

Builders: Fairfield, Glasgow
Yard no: 596
13,465 GRT; 164.0 × 20.2 m /
538 × 66.3 ft; Geared turbines,
Brown-Curtis-Fairfield; Twin
screw; 9,000 SHP; 15, max 16 kn;
Passengers: 516 cabin class, 1,000
3rd class; Crew: 300.

1922 Jan 28: Launched.
1923 Apr: Completed.
Apr 21: Maiden voyage
Glasgow-Montreal.
1933 Passenger accommodation:
314 cabin class, 310 tourist class,
928 3rd class.
1935 Owners changed their name
to Donaldson Atlantic Line.
1939 Sep 3: The *Athenia* was
torpedoed and sunk by the German
submarine *U 30* 200 nautical miles
west of the Hebrides in position
56° 44′N-14° 05′W. 112 dead.
The sinking of the *Athenia*, the
first submarine victim of the
Second World War, was against
the emphatic order that no action
should be taken against passenger
ships for the time being. The
sinking was denied on the German
side during the war.

Turbine steamer *Letitia*
Anchor-Donaldson Line, Glasgow

1946 *Empire Brent*
1951 *Captain Cook*

Builders: Fairfield, Glasgow
Yard no: 601
13,475 GRT; 164.0 × 20.2 m /
538 × 66.3 ft; Geared turbines,
Brown-Curtis-Fairfield; Twin
screw; 9,000 SHP; 15, max 16 kn;
Passengers: 516 cabin class, 1,023
3rd class; Crew: 300.

1924 Oct 14: Launched.
1925 Apr: Completed.
Apr 24: Maiden voyage
Glasgow-Montreal.
1933 Passenger accommodation:
298 cabin class, 310 tourist class,
964 3rd class.
1935 Owners changed their name
to Donaldson Atlantic Line.
1939 Fitted out as armed
merchant cruiser. Later troop
transport.
1944 In service as Canadian
hospital ship.
1946 Sold to British Ministry of
Transport. Management by
Donaldson continued. Renamed
Empire Brent.
Nov 20: Collided with the British
steamer *Stormont*, which sank.

1947 Dec: Overhauled and refitted
as troop transport on the Clyde.
1948 Jul: First voyage on troop
transport service to India and Far
East.
1950 Emigrant service
Glasgow-Sydney.
1951 Jun: Refit as emigrant ship
commenced by Barclay, Curle &
Co at Glasgow, which lasted until
January 1952.
1,088 3rd class passengers. 13,876
GRT. Renamed *Captain Cook*.
1952 Feb 5: First voyage
Glasgow-New Zealand.
1955 Apr: Glasgow-Montreal
service. New Zealand service again
in October after seven round trips.
1960 Apr 29: Arrived at
Inverkeithing. Broken up by T.W.
Ward.

1 *The Anchor liner* Athenia *was the
first ship to be sunk by a submarine
during the Second World War.*
2/3 *The* Athenia's *sister ship, the*
Letitia. *Both photos show the ship in
the '50s as* Captain Cook.

1

2

3

Turbine steamer *Flandria*
Royal Holland Lloyd, Amsterdam

1936 Bretagne

Builders: Barclay, Curle & Co,
Glasgow
Yard no: 594
10,171 GRT; 143.9 × 18.0 m /
472 × 59.1 ft; Geared turbines,
Brown-Curtis-builders; Twin
screw; 6,000 SHP; 14.5 kn;
Passengers: 215 1st class, 110 2nd
class, 1,000 3rd class.

1922 Jun 2: Launched.
Sep: Completed.
Amsterdam-South America
service.
1936 Sold to CGT, Le Havre.
Renamed *Bretagne*. 10,108 GRT.
440 cabin class passengers.
1937 St Nazaire-West Indies
service, later Le Havre-West
Indies.
1939 The *Bretagne* was torpedoed
and sunk by the German
submarine *U 45* 300 nautical miles
from the English Channel in
position 50° 20′N-12° 45′W. Seven
dead.

Turbine steamer *Volendam*
Holland-America Line, Rotterdam

Builders: Harland & Wolff, Govan
Yard no: 649
15,434 GRT; 175.6 × 20.5 m /
472 × 67.3 ft; Geared turbines,
Brown-Curtis-H & W; Twin screw;
8,000 SHP; 15 kn; Passengers: 263
1st class, 436 2nd class, 1,200 3rd
class; Crew: 350.

1922 Jul 6: Launched.
Oct 12: Completed.
Nov 4: Maiden voyage
Rotterdam-New York.
1928 Passenger accommodation:
263 1st class, 428 2nd class, 484
tourist class.
1940 May: Taken over as
transport by the British
Government.
Managed by Cunard Line.
Aug 31: During a voyage Great
Britain-Canada the *Volendam* was
torpedoed while in convoy 300
nautical miles from the Irish coast
by the German submarine *U 60*.
In addition to the crew there were
335 children and 271 adults on
board, who were taken off the

sinking ship by three other
steamers in the convoy. Contrary to
expectations the *Volendam*
remained afloat and was
towed back to Great Britain by the
salvage vessel *Ranger*. (According
to British time the torpedoing
occurred at 23.00 hours on
August 30.)
1941 Jul: In service as troop
transport after repairs by Cammell
Laird at Birkenhead lasting ten
months.
1945 Jul: Handed back to
Holland-America Line, but
chartered by the Ministry of
Transport for a further year as
troop transport.
1946/47 Used as troop transport
Holland-Dutch East Indies and in
emigrant service Rotterdam-
Australia.
1947 Rotterdam-New York service
again. 1,682 passengers in one
class.
1952 Feb: Sold to F. Rijsdijk,
Hendrik Ido Ambacht, to be
broken up.

1/2 *The Royal Holland Lloyd liner*
Flandria, *which came under the CGT
flag in 1936 as the* Bretagné.
3 *The* Volendam, *Holland-America
Line.*

2

3

Turbine steamer *Veendam*
Holland-America Line, Rotterdam

Builders: Harland & Wolff, Govan
Yard no: 650
15,450 GRT; 176.5 × 20.5 m /
579 × 67.3 ft; Geared turbines,
Brown-Curtis-H & W; Twin screw;
8,000 SHP; 15 kn; Passengers: 262
1st class, 436 2nd class, 1,200 3rd
class; Crew: 350.

1922 Nov 18: Launched.
1923 Mar 29: Completed.
Apr 18: Maiden voyage
Rotterdam-New York.
1928 Passenger accommodation
altered. 262 1st class, 430 2nd
class, 480 tourist class. Also used
for cruising.
1939 Sep 17: The *Veendam*
rescued survivors from the British
aircraft carrier *Courageous*, which
had been sunk by the *U 29* in the
Atlantic.
1940 May 11: Badly damaged at
Rotterdam by the fire which spread
from the *Statendam*.
Seized by the German navy.
1941 May 10: Managed by
Hamburg-America Line. Served as
accommodation ship for
submarine crews at Gotenhafen
(Gdynia) and Hamburg.
1945 Badly damaged by bombing
at Hamburg and partially burnt
out.
1946 Jan 15: Returned to
Holland-America Line. To
Amsterdam for repairs.
1947 Jan 30: Placed on New York
service again. Passengers: 223 1st
class, 363 tourist class. 15,652
GRT.
1953 Broken up by Bethlehem
Steel Co, Baltimore.

4/5 *The* Veendam *under the Dutch
flag (4) and serving in the German navy
during the Second World War (5).*

White Star Liner Doric

Turbine steamer *Doric*
White Star Line, Liverpool

Builders: Harland & Wolff, Belfast
Yard no: 573
16,484 GRT; 183.1 × 20.6 m /
601 × 67.6 ft; Geared turbines,
Brown-Curtis-H & W; Twin screw;
9,000 SHP; 15 kn; Passengers: 600
cabin class, 1,700 3rd class; Crew:
350.

1922 Aug 8: Launched.
1923 May 29: Completed.
Jun 8: Maiden voyage
Liverpool-Montreal.
1933 Cruising only.
1934 Cunard Line and White Star
Line amalgamated to form
Cunard-White Star Line.
1935 Sep 5: The *Doric* collided
with the French steamer *Formigny*
in fog off Cape Finisterre. The
Doric was badly damaged but was
able to reach Vigo under her own
steam. After temporary repairs she
sailed to London. She was sold,
after inspection, to J. Cashmore to
be broken up and left for Newport,
Mon, on October 7.

1 *The* Doric *was broken up in 1935 after only twelve years of service.*

Thuringia and Westphalia

Turbine steamer *Thuringia*
Hamburg-America Line,
Hamburg

1930 *General San Martin*
1946 *Empire Deben*

Builders: Howaldt Kiel
Yard no: 610
11,343 GRT; 150.9 × 18.5 m /
495 × 60.7 ft; Geared turbines,
Brown Boverie; Single screw; 5,300
SHP; 13.5 kn; Passengers: 159
cabin class, 652 3rd class; Crew:
164.

1922 Aug 12: Launched. Intended
when ordered in 1917 to be named
Havelland.
1923 Jan 10: Completed.
Jan 22: Maiden voyage
Hamburg-New York.

1930 Refitted for South America
service. 11,251 GRT. Renamed
General San Martin. Passengers:
169 cabin class, 392 3rd class.
1934 Mar 18: Chartered to
Hamburg-South America Line due
to the decentralisation of German
shipping.
1936 Jun 30: Sold to
Hamburg-South America Line.
1940 Jan 22: Accommodation ship
for the German navy. Later,
hospital ship.
1945 Transported 30,000 people
to the west in 11 operations during
the evacuation of the German
Eastern territories.
Oct 8: Handed over to Great
Britain at Copenhagen. Refitted as
troop transport by Deutsche Werft,
Hamburg.

1946 Renamed *Empire Deben*.
Managed for Ministry of Transport
by Shaw, Savill & Albion, London.
1949 Broken up at Newport, Mon.

1 *The* Thuringia *during one of her first*
voyages.

1

2

3

2 *From 1934 the* General San Martin
ex Thuringia *sailed for Hamburg-
South America Line.*
3 *The troop transport* Empire Deben.

Turbine steamer *Westphalia*
Hamburg-America Line,
Hamburg

1930 *General Artigas*

Builders: Howaldt Kiel
Yard no: 611
11,343 GRT; 150.9 × 18.5 m /
495 × 60.7 ft; Geared turbines,
Brown Boverie; Single screw; 5,300
SHP; 13.5 kn; Passengers: 150
cabin class, 652 3rd class; Crew:
164.

1923 Jan 19: Launched. Intended
when ordered in 1917 to be named
Ammerland.
May 17: Completed.
May 21: Maiden voyage
Hamburg-New York.
1926 Jan 31: The Dutch steamer
Alkaid, in distress during a storm
in the Atlantic, radioed an SOS.
The *Westphalia* rescued the
27-man crew.
1929 Refitted for South America
service. 11,254 GRT. Passengers:
169 cabin class, 392 3rd class.
1930 May 1: First voyage
Hamburg-La Plata after being
renamed *General Artigas.*
1934 Nov 8: Chartered to
Hamburg-South America Line due
to the decentralisation of German
shipping.
1936 Jun 30: Sold to
Hamburg-South America Line.
1940 Jan 29: Accommodation ship
for the German navy at Hamburg.
1943 Jul 25: Sunk in Kuhwerder
harbour, Hamburg, during British
air raid.
1946 Wreck raised and scrapped.

4

5

4 *The Hamburg-America Line turbine steamer* Westphalia.
5 *The half-broken up* General Artigas *at Hamburg in 1946.*

Turbine steamer *Cuba*
CGT, St Nazaire

Builders: Swan, Hunter & Wigham Richardson, Newcastle
Yard no: 1108
11,337 GRT; 150.9 × 19.0 m / 495 × 62.3 ft; Geared turbines, Vickers-Rateau-builders; Twin screw; 9,000 SHP; 16 kn; Passengers: 280 1st class, 50 2nd class, 76 3rd class; 680 steerage.

1922 Nov 20: Launched.
1923 Apr: Completed.
May 5: Maiden voyage St Nazaire-West Indies-Vera Cruz.

1940 Oct 31: While on a voyage from Martinique to Casablanca the *Cuba* was stopped and seized by a British warship.
Taken over by British Ministry of War Transport and managed as tranport by Cunard Line. 11,420 GRT.
1945 Apr 6: While sailing in convoy to Le Havre the *Cuba* was torpedoed and sunk by the German submarine *U 1195* in the English Channel in position 50° 36′N-00° 57′W. The *U 1195* was subsequently sunk by the destroyer *Watchman*.

2

1/2 *The* Cuba, *built for the Mexico
service of the CGT.*

Turbine steamer *De Grasse*
CGT, Le Havre

1953 *Empress of Australia*
1956 *Venezuela*

Builders: Cammell Laird & Co,
Birkenhead
Yard no: 886
17,707 GRT; 174.9 × 21.7 m /
574 × 71.2 ft; Geared turbines,
Parsons-builders; Twin screw;
13,000 SHP; 16 kn; Passengers:
399 cabin class, 1,712 3rd class.

1920 Mar 23: Laid down.
Intended name originally *Suffren*.
1924 Feb 23: Launched.
Aug 4: Completed. The final
fitting-out work was carried out at
St Nazaire because of a strike of
British shipyard workers.
Aug 21: Maiden voyage Le
Havre-New York.
1932 18,435 GRT. Passengers:
536 cabin class, 410 3rd class.

1940 Laid up at Bordeaux. Used
as accommodation ship by the
German occupation forces.
1944 Aug 30: Sunk by German
troops during the withdrawal from
Bordeaux.
1945 Aug 30: Raised. Transferred
to St Nazaire and refitted there by
Penhoët.
1947 Jul 12: First post-war voyage
Le Havre-New York. Now only one
funnel. 18,435 GRT. Passengers:
500 cabin class, 470 tourist class.
1951 19,918 GRT.
1952 Apr 24: First voyage Le
Havre-West Indies.
1953 Mar 26: Sold to Canadian
Pacific, London. Passenger
accommodation altered: 220 1st
class, 444 tourist class; 19,379
GRT.
Apr 27: Renamed *Empress of
Australia*.
Apr 28: First voyage
Liverpool-Quebec.

1956 Feb 15: Sold to Sicula
Oceanica, Palermo. Renamed
Venezuela. 18,567 GRT.
Naples-La Guaira service.
1960 Refitted in Italy. Modern,
raked bow. 18,769 GRT. 187.2 m /
614 ft overall length. Passengers:
180 1st class, 500 tourist class, 800
3rd class.
1962 Mar 17: The *Venezuela*
stranded on a rock off Cannes.
Passengers and some of the crew
were taken off the ship.
Apr 16: The ship was refloated.
A subsequent inspection of the
damage indicated that to repair her
would not be economic.
Aug 26: Sold to SA Santa Rosalia,
La Spezia, to be broken up.

2

2 *The* De Grasse *entered service in
1924 after a building time of four years.*
3 *After the refit in 1947 the* De Grasse
had only one funnel.
4 *The former* De Grasse *sailed for
three years for Canadian Pacific as the*
Empress of Australia.
5 *In 1956 the* Empress of Australia *was
bought by Sicula Oceanica and
renamed* Venezuela. *She is shown in
the photo after her refit and
modernisation in 1960.*

3

4

5

München and Stuttgart

Steamship *München*
North German Lloyd, Bremen

1931 *General von Steuben*
1938 *Steuben*

Builders: 'Vulcan', Stettin
Yard no: 669
13,325 GRT; 167.8 × 19.8 m /
551 × 65.0 ft; III exp eng, Vulcan;
Twin screw, 8,500 IHP; 15 kn;
Passengers: 171 1st class, 350 2nd
class, 558 3rd class; Crew: 356.

1922 Nov 25: Launched.
1923 Jun: Completed.
Jun 21: Maiden voyage
Bremerhaven-New York.
1930 Feb 11: Almost completely
burnt out at New York when the
cargo caught fire.
May 9-25: Sailed under own steam
to Bremen after temporary repairs.
Repaired and refitted by AG
'Weser'. 14,690 GRT. Max 10,560
IHP; 16.3 kn with additional low
pressure turbines. Passengers: 214
cabin class, 358 tourist class, 221
3rd class.
Renamed *General von Steuben*.
1931 Jan 20: First voyage after
refit.
1935 Cruising only. 484 1st class
passengers.
1938 Renamed *Steuben*.
1939 Accommodation ship for
Germany Navy at Kiel.
1944 Aug: In the Baltic as
transport for wounded.
1945 Feb 9: The *Steuben* left
Pillau bound for Kiel. On board
were 2,500 wounded, 2,000
refugees and 450 crew.
Feb 10: Shortly before midnight
the Soviet submarine *S 13* sighted
the transport off Stolpmünde and
sank her with two torpedoes. 3,000
dead.

1/2 *The Lloyd steamer* München
*during the '20s (1) and as the cruise
ship* General von Steuben *in 1935 (2).*

1

2

Steamship *Stuttgart*
North German Lloyd, Bremen

Builders: 'Vulcan', Stettin
Yard no: 670
13,325 GRT; 167.8 × 19.8 m /
551 × 65.0 ft; III exp eng, Vulcan;
Twin screw; 8,500 IHP; 15 kn;
Passengers: 171 1st class, 338 2nd
class, 594 3rd class; Crew: 356.

1923 Jul 31: Launched.
1924 Jan: Completed.
Jan 15: Maiden voyage
Bremerhaven-New York.
1937 Cruising only. 13,387 GRT.
1938 Sold to Deutsche
Arbeitsfront (German Labour
Front) as KdF ship. (KdF: Kraft
durch Freude/Strength through
Joy). Management continued
under North German Lloyd. 990
passengers, one class.

1939 Hospital ship for the
Germany Navy.
1943 Oct 9: During the first Allied
air raid on Gotenhafen (Gdynia)
the *Stuttgart,* filled with wounded,
was struck by high-explosive
bombs and was soon ablaze from
end to end. Only a few survivors
could be rescued. The burning
wreck was towed out of the harbour
and sunk at sea with the bodies of
the victims still on board.

3 *The* Stuttgart, *which entered service
in 1924.*

3

4

5

4 *In 1938 the* Stuttgart *was sold to the German Labour Front as a 'Strength through Joy' ship.*
5 *The hospital ship* Stuttgart *at Stettin in 1939.*

Stinnes Liner General Belgrano

Steamship *General Belgrano*
AG Hugo Stinnes, Hamburg

Ex *Bahia Castillo*

Builders: Reiherstiegwerft, Hamburg
Yard no: 446
10,056 GRT; 155.5 × 18.7 m / 510 × 61.4 ft; III exp eng, Reiherstieg; Twin screw: 4,300 IHP; 12, max 12.5 kn; Passengers: 142 2nd class, 542 3rd class; Crew: 165.

1913 Jan 4: Launched as *Bahia Castillo* for Hamburg-South America Line.
Mar 27: Completed. 9,948 GRT. Passengers: 202 2nd class, 2,500 steerage.
Apr: Maiden voyage Hamburg-La Plata ports.
1919 May 22: Handed over to Great Britain. Managed for the Shipping Controller by G. Thompson & Co, London.
1922 Sep: Bought by AG Hugo Stinnes, Hamburg. It was planned to rename the ship *General San Martin,* but after refit she was renamed *General Belgrano* and placed in Hamburg-South America service.
1926 Nov 24: Sold to Hamburg-America Line, which took over the entire Stinnes fleet. The ship remained on the same route. New measurement: 10,121 GRT.
1932 Dec 20: Sold through Treuhand Gesellschaft to the Deutsche Werft, Hamburg, to be broken up.

1/2 *The* General Belgrano *under the
Stinnes flag (1) and as a Hamburg-
America Line steamer about 1930 (2).*

Turbine steamer *Albert Ballin*
Hamburg-America Line,
Hamburg

1935 *Hansa*
1953 *Sovietski Sojus*

Builders: Blohm & Voss, Hamburg
Yard no: 403
20,815 GRT; 191.2 × 22.2 m /
627 × 72.8 ft; Geared turbines, B
& V; Twin screw; 13,500 SHP;
15.5, max 16 kn; Passengers: 251
1st class, 340 2nd class, 960 3rd
class; Crew: 415.

1922 Dec 16: Launched.
1923 Jun 16: Completed.
Jul 4: Maiden voyage
Hamburg-New York.
1930 Mar 11: Trials after refit by
Blohm & Voss. New boilers and
turbines. 29,000 SHP; 19.5 kn;
20,931 GRT.

1934 May 12: During a manoeuvre
at Bremerhaven the North German
Lloyd tugboat *Merkur* came under
the bows of the *Ballin*, and was
forced under the water. Seven
dead.
Jun 6: Trials after second refit by
Blohm & Voss. The forepart was
lengthened and modernised, which
brought a gain of two kn from the
same engine performance. 21,131
GRT; 206.3 m / 677 ft length
overall; Passengers: 204 1st class,
361 tourist class, 400 3rd class.
1935 Oct 1: As a result of pressure
by the National Socialist
government the ship was renamed
Hansa.
1940 Training and
accommodation ship for the
German Navy.
1945 Mar 6: While on an
evacuation voyage from

Gotenhafen (Gdynia) to the
Western Baltic the *Hansa* struck a
mine off Warnemünde. The ship
listed, and the refugees were put
into the boats. During an attempt
to tow the ship away she sank in
shallow water off Warnemünde.
1949 The Soviets raised the wreck.
Refitting and repair work lasted
several years at Antwerp and
Warnemünde.
1953 Renamed *Sovietski Sojus*.
1954 The almost completed ship
was badly damaged by an explosion
and subsequent fire.
1955 Sep: Delivered by
Warnow shipyard to the
Sovtorgflot, Vladivostock. 23,009
GRT. Vladivostock-Kamchatka
service.
1971 Four month general overhaul
at Taikoo Dockyard, Hong Kong.

1

1-5 *The five refitting stages of the Ballin-ships are demonstrated by these pictures of the* Albert Ballin.
(1) Original appearance: Short funnels, open bridge-front, upper hull section painted white.
(2) 1924-25: Lengthened funnels, black hull up to the main deck.
(3) 1927: Glass-enclosed bridge-front.
(4) 1930: Shorter funnels again after engine refit, bridge-front altered (only Albert Ballin *and* Deutschland).
(5) Lengthened forepart after the 1934 refit. Funnels lengthened again.

4

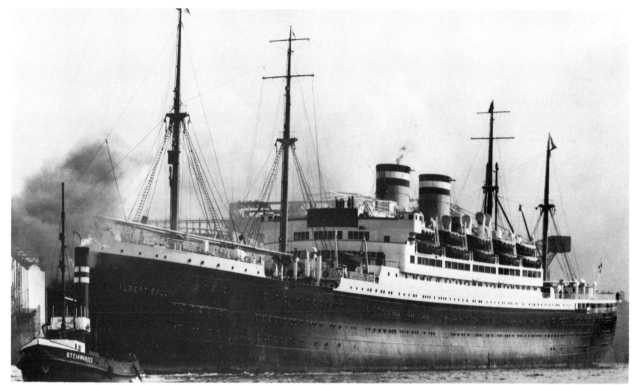

5

6 *The* Hansa *after being raised in 1949.*

7 *The* Sovietski Sojus *ex* Hansa *ex* Albert Ballin.

Turbine steamer *Deutschland*
Hamburg-America Line,
Hamburg

Builders: Blohm & Voss, Hamburg
Yard no: 405
20,607 GRT; 191.2 × 22.2 m /
627 × 72.8 ft; Geared turbines, B
& V; Twin screw; 13,500 SHP;
15.5, max 16 kn; Passengers: 221
1st class; 402 2nd class, 935 3rd
class; Crew: 420.

1923 Apr 28: Launched.
Dec 19: Completed.
1924 Mar 27: Maiden voyage
Hamburg-New York.
1930 May 25: Trials after refit by
Blohm & Voss. New boilers and
turbines. 29,000 SHP; 19.5 kn;
20,742 GRT.
1934 Feb 8: Trials after second
refit by Blohm & Voss. Forepart
lengthened and modernised,
resulting in a gain of two kn from
the same engine performance.
21,046 GRT. 206.3 m / 677 ft
length overall. Passengers: 200 1st
class, 360 tourist class, 400 3rd
class.
1940 Naval accommodation ship
at Gotenhafen (Gdynia).
1945 Evacuated 70,000 people
from the German eastern
territories in seven voyages.
May 3: The *Deutschland* was
attacked and sunk by British
aircraft off Neustadt in the Bay of
Lübeck.
1948 Wreck raised and scrapped.

8

9

8/9 *The* Deutschland *as she appeared around the years 1927 (8) and 1935 (9).*

Turbine steamer *Hamburg*
Hamburg-America Line,
Hamburg

1955 *Yuri Dolgoruki*

Builders: Blohm & Voss, Hamburg
Yard no: 473
21,132 GRT: 193.5 × 22.1 m /
635 × 72.5 ft; Geared turbines, B
& V; Twin screw; 14,000 SHP;
15.5 m max 16.5 kn; Passengers:
222 1st class, 471 2nd class, 456 3rd
class; Crew: 423.

1925 Nov 14: Launched.
1936 Mar 27: Completed.
Apr 9: Maiden voyage
Hamburg-New York.
1929 Aug 31: Refit commenced by
Blohm & Voss, which lasted until
February 6 1930. New boilers and
turbines. 29,000 SHP; 19.5 kn;
21,691 GRT.
1933 Dec 1: Trials after further
refit by Blohm & Voss. Forepart
lengthened and modernised,
resulting in a gain of two kn from
the same engine performance.
22,117 GRT. 206.5 m / 677 ft
length overall. Passengers: 200 1st
class, 350 tourist class, 400 3rd
class.
1940 Naval accommodation ship
at Gotenhafen (Gdynia).
1945 The ship transported 23,000
people to the West in three voyages
during the evacuation of the
German Eastern territories.
Mar 7: The *Hamburg* disembarked
her refugees at Sassnitz. While
being towed to another anchorage
she struck two mines and sank.
1950 Raised by Soviet salvors.
Repaired and refitted at
Warnemünde and Antwerp.
1955 Renamed *Yuri Dolgoruki*.

Work on the almost completely
reconstructed passenger ship
halted.
1957 The Warnow shipyard,
Warnemünde, began a conversion
to whaling mother-ship.
1960 Jul: Delivered to Soviet State
shipping line. 25,377 GRT. Home
port Kaliningrad.

10/11 *The* Hamburg *after her 1930
refit* (*10*) *and after the lengthening of
the forecastle in 1933* (*11*).
12 *The Soviet whaling mother-ship*
Yuri Dolgoruki *ex* Hamburg.

10

11

12

Turbine steamer *New York*
Hamburg-America Line,
Hamburg

Builders: Blohm & Voss, Hamburg
Yard no: 474
21,455 GRT; 193.5 × 22.1 m /
635 × 72.5 ft; Geared turbines, B
& V; Twin screw; 14,000 SHP;
15.5, max 16.5 kn; Passengers: 247
1st class, 321 2nd class, 464 3rd
class; Crew: 420.

1926 Oct 20: Launched.
1927 Mar 12: Completed.
Apr 1: Maiden voyage
Hamburg-New York.
1930 Apr 16: Trials after refit by
Blohm & Voss. New turbines;
29,000 SHP; 19.5 kn; 21,867
GRT.
1934 Mar: Second refit by Blohm
& Voss completed. Forepart
lengthened and modernised,
resulting in a gain of two kn from
the same engine performance.

22,337 GRT; 206.5 m / 677 ft
length overall. Passengers: 210 1st
class, 350 tourist class, 400 3rd
class.
Dec 18: While homeward-bound
for Hamburg the *New York*
received an SOS call from the
Norwegian cargo vessel *Sisto*,
which was drifting and sinking in
a hurricane. She reached the
damaged ship by evening, to find
the British tanker *Mobiloil* already
on the scene. Four more passenger
ships approached, including the
German liners *Europa* and
Gerolstein. Because of the
persisting storm it was decided to
postpone the rescue until the
following morning. The *Sisto* now
began to sink more quickly. With
great difficulty, the *New York*
lowered a boat and the Norwegian
crew was rescued.
1936 May 7: Collision in fog in the
channel with the Dutch steamer

Alphard, which immediately sank.
New York rescued the crew.
1939 Aug 28: Because of the threat
of war the ship left New York
without passengers or cargo. On
the outbreak of war she made for
Murmansk, arriving there on
September 5.
Dec 13: Arrived at Hamburg from
Murmansk.
1940 Naval accommodation ship
at Kiel.
1945 Used in the evacuation of the
German eastern territories.
Apr 3: The *New York* was hit by
two bombs at Kiel and capsized on
fire.
1949 Mar 21: The wreck was
raised and towed to Great Britain
to be scrapped.

13

14

15

13/14 *The* New York *in 1933 (13) and after her 1934 refit (14).*
15 *The burnt out and capsized* New York *at Kiel in 1945.*

Minnewaska and Minnetonka

Turbine steamer *Minnewaska*
Atlantic Transport Line, Belfast

Builders: Harland & Wolff, Belfast
Yard no: 613
21,716 GRT; 190.8 × 24.5 m /
626 × 80.4 ft; Geared turbines,
Brown-Curtis-H & W; Twin screw;
16,000 SHP; 16, max 17.8 kn;
Passengers: 369 1st class.

1923 Mar 22: Launched.
Aug 25: Completed.
Sep 1: Maiden voyage London-New
York.
1932 May 27: First voyage
Antwerp-New York under charter
to Red Star Line.
1933 Oct: Laid up.
1934 Sold to be broken up by
Douglas & Ramsay, Port Glasgow.

Turbine steamer *Minnetonka*
Atlantic Transport Line, Belfast

Builders: Harland & Wolff, Belfast
Yard no: 614
21,998 GRT; 190.8 × 24.5 m /
626 × 80.4 ft; Geared turbines,
Brown-Curtis-H & W; Twin screw;
16,000 SHP; 16, max 17.6 kn;
Passengers: 369 1st class.

1924 Jan 10: Launched.
Apr 24: Completed.
May 3: Maiden voyage
London-New York.
1933 Oct: Laid up.
1934 Nov: Sold to Douglas &
Ramsay to be broken up. Scrapped
at Bo'ness.

3

1-3 *The turbine steamers* Minnewaska
(1 & 3) and Minnetonka *(2), built in
1923/24, were sold to be broken up ten
years later.*

Steamship *Sierra Ventana*
North German Lloyd, Bremen

1935 *Sardegna*

Builders: Bremer Vulkan,
Vegesack
Yard no: 610
11,392 GRT; 155.7 × 18.8 m /
511 × 61.7 ft; III exp eng, Vulkan;
Twin screw; 6,400 IHP; 14, max
14.5 kn; Passengers: 222 1st class,
179 2nd class, 712 3rd class; Crew:
264.

1923 May 16: Launched.
Aug 30: Completed.
Sep 8: Maiden voyage
Bremerhaven-New York. Used in
New York or La Plata service.
1935 Sold to 'Italia' Flotta
Riunite, Genoa. Renamed
Sardegna. South America service.
Troop transport.
1937 Sold to Lloyd Triestino,
Trieste.
1940 Dec 29: Torpedoed by the
Greek submarine *Proteus* off
Valona while on a troop transport
voyage from that port to Brindisi.

She sank in position 40° 31′N-
19° 02′E. The Italian torpedo-boat
Antares rammed the submarine
which sank.

Steamship *Sierra Córdoba*
North German Lloyd, Bremen

Builders: Bremer Vulkan,
Vegesack
Yard no: 611
11,469 GRT; 155.7 × 18.8 m /
511 × 61.7 ft; III exp eng, Vulkan;
Twin screw; 6,400 IHP; 14, max
14.5 kn; Passengers: 160 1st class,
1,143 3rd class, 762 steerage;
Crew: 300.

1923 Sep 26: Launched.
1924 Jan 19: Completed.
Jan 26: Maiden voyage
Bremerhaven-La Plata ports.
Cruising.
1935 Sold to German Labour
Front, and managed by North
German Lloyd for 'Strength
through Joy' trips. 1,000 tourist

class passengers. 11,492 GRT.
1940 Naval accommodation ship
at Kiel.
1945 May: British war prize.
Accommodation ship at Hamburg.
1946 Jan 13: Completely burnt
out. Three dead.
1948 Jan 18: While being towed
from Hamburg to the Clyde, where
the ship was to be broken up, the
hawsers broke. The *Sierra Córdoba*
drifted out of sight of the towing
vessel. The wreck stranded off
Esbjerg and sank in position
55° 50′N-07° 30′E.

1

1/2 *The* Sierra Ventana (*1*) *became the Italian liner* Sardegna (*2*) *in 1935.*
3 *Steamship* Sierra Córdoba.

2

3

Steamship *Sierra Morena*
North German Lloyd, Bremen

1934 *Der Deutsche*
1946 *Asia*

Builders: Bremer Vulkan,
Vegesack
Yard No: 612
11,430 GRT; 155.7 × 18.8 m /
511 × 61.7 ft; III exp eng, Vulkan;
Twin screw; 6,400 IHP; 14, max
14.5 kn; Passengers: 157 1st class,
1,145 3rd class, 763 steerage;
Crew: 298.

1924 Jun 3: Launched.
Oct 10: Completed.
Oct 25: Maiden voyage

Bremerhaven-La Plata ports.
Cruising.
1934 Jul 20: Renamed *Der
Deutsche*. Cruising only. 11,453
GRT. 1,000 tourist class
passengers.
1935 Sold to German Labour
Front; management continued
under North German Lloyd.
Cruising for 'Strength through
Joy'.
1940 Transport for German navy.
Later, accommodation ship at
Königsberg and Gotenhafen
(Gdynia).
1945 Transport for the wounded.
Der Deutsche brought 34,500

refugees to the west in the
evacuation of the German eastern
territories.
May 3: Hit by bomb off Fehmarn;
ship beached. Later towed to
Kiel.
1946 Mar 18: Awarded to the
Soviet Union as war prize.
Renamed *Asia*. Repaired and
refitted at Warnemünde by the
Warnow shipyard.
1950 Jun: Placed in service by the
Soviet state shipping line. 12,019
GRT. Used in Far Eastern waters.
1970 Out of Lloyd's Register.

4

5

6

4/5 *The* Sierra Morena (*4*) *was refitted for cruising in 1934 and renamed* Der Deutsche (*5*).
6 *In June 1950 the* Asia *was taken over by the Soviet state shipping line.*

Talma and Tilawa

Steamship *Talma*
British India Line, Glasgow

Builders: Hawthorn, Leslie & Co,
Newcastle
Yard no: 529
10,000 GRT; 143.6 × 18.1 m /
471 × 59.4 ft; IV exp eng from
builders; Single screw: 5,000 IHP;
13 kn; Passengers: 135 1st and 2nd
class, approx. 1,000 Asiatic
steerage passengers: Crew: 220

1923 Jun 14: Launched.
Sep 12: Completed. In service
between Calcutta and Japan.
1949 Apr 14: Left Bombay in tow
of salvage vessel *Twyford*.
May 29: Arrived Inverkeithing.
Broken up.

Steamship *Tilawa*
British India Line, Glasgow

Builders: Hawthorn, Leslie & Co,
Newcastle
Yard no: 530
10,006 GRT; 143.6 × 18.1 m /
471 × 59.4 ft; IV exp eng from
builders; Single screw; 5,000 IHP;
13 kn; Passengers: 135 1st and 2nd
class, approx. 1,000 Asiatic
steerage passengers; Crew: 220.

1924 Feb 20: Launched.
May 1: Completed. In service
between Calcutta and Japan.
1942 Nov 23: While on a voyage
from Bombay to Mombasa the
Tilawa was torpedoed in the early
morning by the Japanese
submarine *I 29*. Panic broke out
among the steerage passengers,
which led to unnecessary loss of life
when the boats and rafts were
lowered. After one hour the *Tilawa*
was still afloat without any
recognisable sign of having been

hit. Just as the crew and passengers
wanted to go on board the ship
again, she was hit by a second
torpedo, and sank in position
8° 36′N-61° 08′E. 280 dead.

1

1/2 *The sister ships* Talma (1) *and*
Tilawa (2), *built for the British India
Line's India-Japan service.*
3 *The* Talma *during trials.*
4 *The* Tilawa *during the Second World
War.*

2

3

4

Turbine steamer *Slamat*
Rotterdam Lloyd, Rotterdam

Builders: 'De Schelde', Vlissingen
Yard no: 176
11,406 GRT; 155.8 × 18.9 m /
511 × 62.0 ft; Geared turbines,
Parsons-'De Schelde': Twin screw;
7,000 SHP; 15 kn; Passengers: 150
1st class, 180 2nd class, 70 3rd
class.

1923 Oct 27: Launched. Intended
name originally *Papandajan*.
1924 Apr 12: Completed.
Rotterdam-Batavia service.

1931 Refitted at Wilton's,
Rotterdam. New Maierform
forepart. Turbines rebuilt. 9,200
SHP; 17.5 kn; 11,636 GRT; 161.5
m / 530 ft length overall.
Oct 7: First voyage after refit.
1940 Placed under British control
as transport after the Dutch
capitulation.
1941 Apr 27: In the course of the
British evacuation from Greece the
Slamat had taken British soldiers
on board. The ship was attacked by
German aircraft off Nauplia and
sunk. 700 survivors out of her total

complement of 900 were picked up
by the destroyers *Diamond* and
Wryneck. In the continuing
German air attacks both of these
destroyers were sunk, whereby 650
of the *Slamat* survivors lost their
lives.

1 *Turbine steamer* Slamat, *original
external appearance.*
2 *In 1931 the* Slamat *received a
Maierform forepart.*

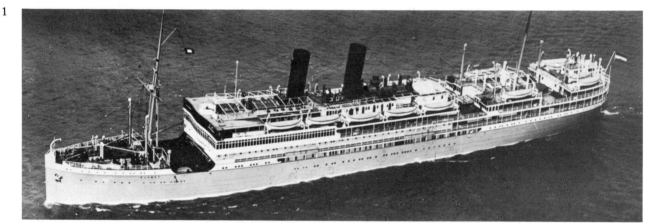

Motor vessel *Indrapoera*
Rotterdam Lloyd, Rotterdam

1956 *Assuncion*
1957 *Bianca C*
1958 *Melanesien*

Builders: 'De Schelde', Vlissingen
Yard no: 178
10,772 GRT; 152.2 × 18.3 m /
499 × 60.0 ft; Sulzer-Diesel, 'De
Schelde'; Twin screw; 7,000 BHP;
15 kn; Passengers: 141 1st class,
184 2nd class, 68 3rd class.

1925 Mar 21: Launched. Intended
name originally *Wajang*.

1926 Jan 30: Completed.
Feb 10: Maiden voyage
Rotterdam-Batavia.
1931 Sep: Refitted at Rotterdam.
New Sulzer Diesels from 'De
Schelde'. 9,000 BHP; 17 kn. New
forepart. Length overall now 154.8
m / 508 ft; 10,746 GRT.
1933 Nov 27: Superstructure badly
damaged by fire at Rotterdam.
10,825 GRT after repairs.
1940 Transport under British
control until 1947.
Registered at Willemstad until
1948.

1948/49 Refit. Cargo capacity
increased. Accommodation for 96
passengers 1st class. 9,585 GRT.
1956 Sold to Providencia Shipping
Co, Panama. Renamed *Assuncion*.
Resold to G. Gosta fu Andrea,
Genoa.
1957 Renamed *Bianca C*.
1958 Chartered to Messageries
Maritimes. Renamed *Melanesien*.
Marseille-Sydney service.
1963 Oct: Broken up in Italy.

3/4 The Indrapoera *before (3) and
after (4) her refit in 1949.*

3

4

Motor vessel *Sibajak*
Rotterdam Lloyd, Rotterdam

Builders: 'De Schelde', Vlissingen
Yard no: 181
12,040 GRT; 161.5 × 19.1 m /
530 × 627 ft; Sulzer-Diesel, 'De
Schelde'; Twin screw; 10,200 BHP;
17 kn; Passengers: 527 in three
classes; Crew 209.

1927 Apr 2: Launched.
Dec: Completed.
1928 Feb 8: Maiden voyage
Rotterdam-Batavia.
1935 Passenger accommodation
modernised. 12,226 GRT.
1940 Registered at Willemstad,
Curacao, until 1948. Troop
transport under P & O
management.
1950 First voyage in emigrant
service Rotterdam-Sydney.
1951 Rotterdam-Indonesia service
again.
1952 Apr: First voyage
Rotterdam-Quebec.

May: First voyage Rotterdam-New
York.
1953 12,342 GRT.
1955 Rotterdam-Indonesia service
again.
1959 Aug 25: Arrived at Hong
Kong to be broken up.

5 *The* Sibajak, *built in 1927.*

5

Bibliography and Acknowledgements

Periodicals
Germanischer Lloyd, Register (Berlin, Hamburg) from 1912
Lloyd's Register of Shipping (London) from 1912
Weyer's Taschenbuch der Kriegsflotten (Munich) from 1914

Magazines
Die Seekiste (Kiel) 1950-1964
Engineering (London) 1912-1925
Fairplay (London) 1913-1919
International Marine Engineering (New York) 1912-1930
Marine News (Kendal) 1950-1972
Motorship (New York) 1921-1932
Schiffbau (Berlin) 1912-1939
Sea Breezes (Liverpool) 1949-1973
Shipbuilding and Shipping Record (London) 1918-1930
The Belgian Shiplover (Brussels) 1959-1972
The Marine Engineer (London) 1912-1914
The Shipbuilder (London and Newcastle) 1912-1937

Books
Anderson, *White Star* (Prescot) 1964
Bonsor, *North Atlantic Seaway* (Prescot) 1955
de Boer, *The Centenary of the Stoomvaart Maatschappij 'Nederland' 1870-1970* (Kendal) 1970
Dunn, *Famous Liners of the Past, Belfast Built* (London) 1964
Hocking, *Dictionary of Disasters at Sea during the Age of Steam* (London) 1969
Hümmelchen, *Handelsstörer* (Munich) 1967
Isherwood, *Steamers of the Past* (Liverpool)
Jentschura-Jung-Mickel, *Die japanischen Kriegsschiffe 1869-1945* (Munich) 1970
Kludas, *Die grossen deutschen Passagierschiffe* (Oldenburg and Hamburg) 1971
Le Fleming, *Blue Funnel Line* (Southampton) 1961
Maber, *North Star to Southern Cross* (Prescot) 1967
Musk, *Canadian Pacific* (London) 1968
Rohwer, *Die U-Boot Erfolge der Achsenmächte 1939-1945* (Munich) 1968

Rohwer-Hümmelchen, *Chronik des Seekrieges 1939-1945* (Oldenburg and Hamburg) 1968

Other sources
Archives and publications of shipyards and shipping lines; statements and reports in newspapers.

I should like to register my very sincere thanks for the kind loan of photographs. The pictures in this book were obtained from the following sources:

Marius Bar, Toulon, pages 19/1, 21/2 & 3, 159/6 & 7
Blohm + Voss AG, Hamburg, pages 10/4, 12/8, 13/9, 34/3, 35/4, 218/4
Bremer Vulkan, Bremen-Vegesack, pages 69/1 & 2, 230/4
Canadian Pacific Steamships Ltd, London, pages 15/2, 49/2, 71/1 & 2, 97/1, 99/4, 145/1 & 2, 147/3 & 5, 209/4
Compagnie Générale Transatlantique, Paris, pages 65/1 & 2, 67/3, 207/1, 208/2
Cunard Steam-Ship Co Ltd, pages 17/1 & 2, 125/3 139/4, 169/5, 236/4
Det Forenede Dampskibs-Selskab A/S, Copenhagen, page 31/1
A. Duncan, Gravesend, pages 18/4 & 5, 37/1, 55/2, 61/1, 77/1, 89/5, 93/2, 105/1, 123/3 & 4, 125/2, 129/2, 133/6, 136/3, 141/5, 147/4, 150/3, 162/5, 163/8, 167/1 & 2, 170/6, 171/8, 173/2 & 3, 175/4 & 5, 177/2, 185/2, 187/4 & 5, 191/3, 197/3, 223/12
Laurence Dunn, Gravesend, pages 39/3, 41/5 & 6, 43/2, 74/1, 79/3, 121/2, 126/4, 127/5, 151/4, 195/3, 203/3, 209/5
Ellerman Lines Ltd, London, page 181/2 & 3
Hans Graf, Hamburg, pages 13/10 39/1, 57/4 & 5, 61/2, 63/1 & 2, 76/3, 95/3, 117/12, 131/3, 155/2, 157/4, 160/3, 177/1, 182/1, 195/2, 232/1
Hapag-Lloyd AG, Hamburg and Bremen, pages 2, 9/2, 46/3, 47/4 & 5, 48/1, 53/8, 211/1 & 2, 212/3, 216/1,

218/5, 221/9, 223/10 & 11, 224/13, 228/1
Hans Hartz, Hamburg, pages 193/4, 203/2, 225/14, 231/5
E.K. Haviland, Baltimore, page 25/5
F.W. Hawks, Horsham, pages 87/2, 127/6, 183/2
Historisch Topograf Atlas, Amsterdam, pages 52/6, 196/1
Imperial War Museum, London, pages 27/3, 171/7
'Italia' SpA di Nav, Genoa, pages 83/6, 104/4
Dr D. Jung, Berlin, pages 29/3, 104/6, 155/3, 199/5, 205/5, 213/5, 219/6, 225/15
J.F. Horst Koenig, Hamburg, page 157/5
A. Lagendijk, Enschede, pages 23/2, 95/4
K.P. Lewis, Bromborough, pages 50, 169/5
Lloyd Triestino, Trieste, pages 89/6 96/2, 103/3, 104/5
Mariners Museum, Newport News, pages 111/6, 115/9
Dr J. Meyer, Rellingen, pages 51/4, 53/7, 202/1, 229/3
National Maritime Museum, London, page 16/3
Norske Amerikalinje A/S, Oslo, page 100/1
Peninsular and Oriental Steam Navigation Co, London, pages 54/1, 72/1, 73/2 & 3, 91/1, 149/1, 188/6, 189/7 & 8, 233/2-4
P.E.R. Scarceriaux, Brussels, pages 25/4, 115/11
K.-H. Schwadtke, Berlin, page 45/2
H. v Seggern, Hamburg, page 213/4
Shaw, Savill & Albion Co Ltd, London, page 183/3
United States Lines, Inc, New York, pages 11/15, 119/13
All other photographs are from the author's collection.